VEGAN COOKBOOK WITH 50 QUICK & EASY RECIPES

A STEP-BY-STEP EASY HEALTHY FOOD GUIDE FOR A HEALTHY DIET

BY

STEF HARRISON

Contents

Curried Tomato Tortellini Soup Recipe 13

Sparkling Cranberries 16

The Best Simple Cauliflower Soup 18

Sunshine Pad Thai (Vegetarian) 21

Vibrant Tasty Green Beans 24

Great Vegetarian Poke Bowl 26

Vegetarian Split Pea Soup 28

Meyer Lemon Focaccia 30

Green Falafel Bowl 33

Quick-Pickled Zucchini 36

Simple Sautéed Zucchini Recipe 39

An Amazing Vegetarian Paella 41

Berry Swirl Ice Cream (Vegan, Dairy-Free) 44

Grilled Zucchini & Bread Salad 47

Sriracha Rainbow Noodle Salad 50

Roasted Tomato Salsa 53

Lively Up Yourself Lentil Soup Recipe 55

Lime & Blistered Peanut Coleslaw 58

Avocado Asparagus Tartine 61

Simple Asparagus Soup 63

Rhubarb & Rosewater Syrup 66

A Few Words on How to Cook Artichokes 68

The Creamiest Vegan Soup (Cauliflower) 72

How to Make the Creamy, Toasted Coconut Milk of Your Dreams 74

The Ultimate Vegan Nachos 76

Mushroom Scallion Tartine with Poblano Yogurt 78

Turmeric Cashews 80

A California Panzanella 82

Make-Ahead Vegan Samosa Shepherd's Pie 84

This is How You Step Up Your Guacamole Game 87

Magic Sauce 89

Simple Brown Rice Sushi Bowl 91

Orange Pan-Glazed Tempeh 93

Make-Ahead Super Green Vegan Quinoa Burritos 96

Broccoli Cheddar Soup 98

Golden-Crusted Sesame-Seeded Tofu 101

Weeknight Ponzu Pasta 103

An Immunity Soup to Light up Your Insides 106

A Glow-Promoting, Luminizing Breakfast Beauty Bowl 108

Ribollita, the Tuscan Stew You Should Be Eating Regularly 110

Last-Minute Red Lasagna 113

CAP Beauty No-Bone Broth 116

Golden Beet Hummus 119

Instant Pot Mushroom Stroganoff with Vodka 122

Quick Vegan Enchiladas with Sweet Potato Sauce 125

White Bean Soup with Pesto Herb Dumplings 128

Instant Pot Chickpea Cauliflower Korma 131

Winter Green Miso Paste 133

Instant Pot Minestrone Soup 135

Vegetable Noodle Soup 138

Caramelised Tofu 141

Goth Hummus 143

California Tom Yum Soup 145

Five-Minute Avocado Dressing with Herbs and Spinach .. 147

Coconut Red Lentil Soup 149

The Vegan Diet

The veggie diet has gotten famous. An increasing number of individuals have chosen to become vegetarian for moral, ecological, or wellness reasons. When done right, such an eating routine can bring about different medical advantages, including a trimmer waistline and improved glucose control. Yet an eating regimen dependent on plant-based foods may sometimes actually increase the risk of nutrient deficiencies.

What Is a Vegan Diet?

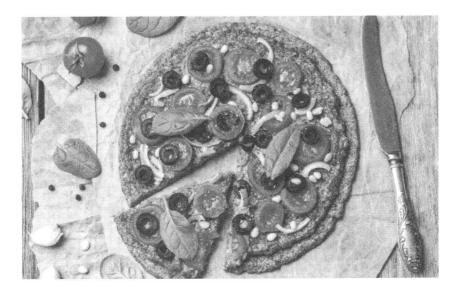

Veganism is a method of living that endeavors to avoid all types of animal abuse and cruelty, regardless of whether for nourishment, clothing, or some other reason. Hence, a vegan diet is without any animal products, including meat, eggs, and dairy.

1

Various Types of Vegan Diets

There is an assortment of veggie diets. The most widely recognized include:

- **Whole-food veggie lover diet:** An eating regimen dependent on a wide variety of entire plant food sources; for example, natural products, vegetables, entire grains, vegetables, nuts, and seeds.
- **Raw-food vegetarian diet:** A veggie lover diet dependent on raw natural products, vegetables, nuts, seeds, and other plant-based sources prepared at temperatures below 118°F (48°C).
- **80/10/10**: The 80/10/10 eating regimen is a raw-food vegetarian diet that breaking points fat-rich plants; for example, nuts and avocados, which depend mostly on the raw products of soil greens. This is also referred to as the low-fat, raw food veggie lover diet, or fruitarian diet.
- **The starch solution**: A low-fat, high-carb veggie lover diet similar to the 80/10/10 diet; however, this one focuses on cooked starches like potatoes, rice, and corn, rather than raw foods.
- **Raw till 4**: A low-fat veggie lover diet propelled by the 80/10/10 and starch solution. Raw foods are eaten until 4 p.m., with the alternative of a prepared plant-based meal for dinner.

- **The thrive diet:** The thrive diet is a raw food vegetarian diet. Followers eat only plant-based meals that are raw or negligibly cooked at low temperatures.
- **Junk-nourishment vegetarian diet**: A veggie lover diet ailing in entire plant nourishments that depends intensely on mock meats and cheeses, fries, vegetarian pastries, and other vigorously prepared vegetarian food sources.

Although more varieties of the veggie lover diet exist, most scientific research only rarely distinguishes between the various types of vegetarian diets.

Veggie lover Diets Can Help You Lose Weight

Veggie lovers will, in general, be more slender and have a lower body mass index (BMI) than non-vegetarians. This may explain why an increasing number of individuals go vegetarian or vegan as an approach to losing excess weight. Some portion of the weight-related changes vegetarians experience might be explained by factors other than diet. These may include a more advantageous way of life choice; for example, physical activity or other wellness-related practices.

In any case, a few randomized controlled trials, which controlled for these outside elements, report that vegetarians eat fewer carbs, which is more conducive to weight reductions than the eating regimens they are contrasted with. Strikingly, the weight reduction advantage perseveres even when the control group eats fewer carbs as well. These incorporate weight control plans prescribed by the American Dietetic Association (ADA), the American Heart Association (AHA), and the National Cholesterol Education Program (NCEP). Furthermore, the researchers generally report that participants on vegetable-based diets lose more weight than those following calorie-confined diets, even when they are permitted to eat until they feel full. The characteristic propensity to eat fewer calories on a veggie-lover diet might be brought about by a higher dietary fibre intake, which can make one feel fuller.

Veggie lover Diets, Blood Sugar and Type 2 Diabetes

Embracing a vegetarian diet may help hold one's glucose in line as well, therefore keeping type 2 diabetes under control. A few experiments show that vegetarians enjoy lower glucose levels, higher insulin affectability, and up to a 78% lower risk of developing type 2 diabetes than non-vegetarians. A veggie lover's weight loss may additionally add to the diet's capacity to bring down glucose levels.

Veggie lover Diets and Heart Health

A veggie lover diet may help keep your heart healthy. Observational investigations report vegetarians may have up to a 75% lower risk of growing hypertension and 42% lower risk of dying from heart disease. Randomized controlled investigations, the rigorous type of experiments, add to the evidence.

A few reports that veggie lovers' calorie counts are considerably more viable at decreasing glucose, LDL, and absolute cholesterol than abstinence from the food they are contrasted with. These impacts could be particularly valuable since lowering blood pressure, cholesterol, and blood sugar may reduce coronary illness risk by up to 46%.

Other Health Benefits of Vegan Diets

Veggie lovers' intake of fewer calories is connected to a variety of other medical advantages, including benefits for:

Cancer risk: Vegans may benefit from a 15% lower risk of passing away from this disease.

Arthritis: Vegans who eat fewer carbs appear to be especially adept at decreasing manifestations of joint pain; for example, joint swelling and morning solidness.

Kidney function: Diabetics who substitute meat for plant protein may diminish their risk of poor kidney work.

Alzheimer's disease: Observational investigations show that parts of the vegetarian diet may help lessen the risk of building up Alzheimer's illness.

Remember that the greater part of the evidence supporting these advantages is observational. It makes it hard to decide if the vegetarian diet straightforwardly caused the benefits. More randomized controlled trials are required before strong conclusions can be made.

Foods to Avoid

Vegetarians abstain from eating any animal foods, just as any food sources containing fixings got from animals. These include:

Meat and poultry: Beef, lamb, pork, veal, horse, organ meat, wild meat, chicken, turkey, goose, duck, quail, and so forth.

Fish and seafood: All kinds of fish, anchovies, shrimp, squid, scallops, calamari, mussels, crab, lobster, and so on.

Dairy: Milk, yogurt, cheddar, margarine, cream, ice cream, and so on.

Eggs: From chickens, quails, ostriches, fish, and so forth.

Bee products: Honey, honeybee dust, imperial jam, and so on.

Animal-based fixings: Whey, casein, lactose, egg white egg whites, gelatin, cochineal or carmine, isinglass, shellac, L-cysteine, animal-derived nutrient D3 and fish-derived omega-3 fatty fats.

Foods to Eat

Health-conscious veggie lovers substitute animal products with plant-based products, for example:

Tofu, tempeh and seitan: These are flexible protein-rich options that can be used as substitutes for meat, fish, poultry, and eggs in numerous recipes.

Legumes: Beans, lentils, and peas are amazing wellsprings of numerous supplements and helpful plant mixes. Growing, fermenting, and appropriate cooking can build supplement retention.

Nuts and nut butters: Especially the unblanched and unroasted varieties, which are great wellsprings of iron, fiber, magnesium, zinc, selenium, and vitamin E.

Seeds: Especially hemp, chia, and flaxseeds, which all contain a decent measure of protein and advantageous omega-3 fatty acids.

Calcium-fortified plant milk and yoghurts: These assist vegetarians with reaching their prescribed dietary calcium intakes. Choose those additionally strengthened with vitamins B12 and D whenever possible.

Algae: Spirulina and chlorella are great sources of complete protein. Different varieties are extraordinary sources of iodine.

Nourishing yeast: This is a simple method to build the protein substance of vegetarian dishes and includes an intriguing cheesy flavor. Pick vitamin B12-fortified assortments if possible.

Whole grains, oats, and pseudocereals: These are an incredible wellspring of complex carbs, fiber, iron, B-vitamins, and a few minerals. Spelt, teff, amaranth, and quinoa are particularly high-protein choices.

Grown and aged plant nourishments: Ezekiel bread, tempeh, miso, natto, sauerkraut, pickles, kimchi, and kombucha (fermented tea) regularly contain probiotics and vitamin K2. Growing and ageing can likewise help improve mineral absorption.

Fruits and vegetables: Both are extraordinary foods to build your nutrient intake. Leafy greens, for example, bok choy, spinach, kale, watercress, and mustard greens are especially high in iron and calcium.

Risks and How to Minimize Them

Favoring a well-arranged eating regimen that rejects prepared foods and replaces them with nutrient-rich ones is important for everybody, not just vegetarians. That following ill-conceived veggie-lover eats fewer carbs are especially in the risk of certain supplement inadequacies. Studies show that vegetarians are at a greater danger of lacking sufficient blood levels of vitamin B12, vitamin D, long-chain omega-3s, iodine, iron, calcium, and zinc Not getting enough of these supplements is troubling for everybody, except it might represent a specific hazard to those with expanded prerequisites, for example, kids or women who are pregnant or breastfeeding. Your genetic makeup and the makeup of your gut microbes may likewise impact your capacity to determine the supplements you need from a vegetarian diet.

Fortified foods, particularly those with added calcium, vitamin D, and vitamin B12, ought to likewise show up on your plate. Besides, veggie lovers needing to improve their retention of iron and zinc. Also, the inclusion of seaweed or iodized salt to the eating regimen can assist veggie lovers with arriving at their suggested everyday intake of iodine.

In conclusion, omega-3-containing foods, particularly those high in alpha-linolenic acid (ALA), can enable the body to create longer-chain omega-3s; for example, eicosapentaenoic acid (EPA) and docosahexaenoic acid (DHA). Foods high in ALA include chia, hemp, flaxseeds, pecans, and soybeans. However, there's a discussion concerning whether even eating these foods is enough to address daily issues. In this way, a daily intake of 200–300 mg of EPA and DHA from a green growth oil supplement might be a more secure approach to avoid low levels.

Supplements to Consider

A few veggie lovers may think that it's hard to eat enough of the nutrient-rich or fortified nourishments above to meet their day-by-day needs. In this situation, the following enhancements can be especially beneficial:

Vitamin B12: Vitamin B12 in cyanocobalamin form is the most studied and appears to function well for the vast majority.

Vitamin D: Opt for D2 or vegetarian D3 structures; for example, those produced by Nordic Naturals or Viridian.

EPA and DHA: Sourced from algae oil.

Iron: Should only be enhanced on account of a tested lack, as ingesting an excessive amount of iron from enhancements can cause health difficulties and forestall the retention of different nutrients.

Iodine: Take a supplement or include 1/2 teaspoon of iodised salt to your eating routine every day.

Calcium: Calcium is best consumed when taken in dosages of 500 mg or less at once. Take calcium simultaneously, as iron or zinc supplements may decrease their retention.

Zinc: Taken in zinc gluconate or zinc citrate structures. Not to be taken simultaneously with calcium supplements.

The most effective method to Eat Vegan at Restaurants

Dining out as a vegetarian, or especially as a vegan, can be testing. One approach to decrease pressure is to research vegetarian-friendly cafés early, for example on Web sites like Happycow or Vegguide. Mobile applications like VeganXpress and Vegman may likewise be useful. When eating in a non-vegetarian-friendly establishment, take a stab at filtering the menu online in advance to gather what vegetarian choices they may have for you.

Once in a while, calling early enables the chef to create something particularly for you. It allows you to arrive at the restaurant sure that you'll have something more fascinating than a side serving of mixed greens to eat. If all else fails, settle on ethnic restaurants. They will, in general, have dishes that are normally vegetarian-friendly or can be effectively adjusted to be so. Mexican, Thai, Middle Eastern, Ethiopian, and Indian restaurants will usually be great choices. Another simple tip is to arrange a few vegetarian appetizers or side dishes to make up a whole meal.

Healthy Vegan Snacks

Snacks are a great method to remain empowered and keep hunger under control between meals. Some intriguing, versatile veggie options include:

- Vegetables with a bit of nut butter
- Hummus
- Dietary yeast sprinkled on popcorn
- Broiled chickpeas
- Nut and natural product bars
- Trail mix
- Chia pudding
- Handcrafted biscuits
- Whole wheat pita with salsa and guacamole
- Cereal with plant milk
- Edamame
- Whole grain wafers and cashew nut spread
- A plant milk latte or cappuccino
- Dried seaweed snacks

When arranging a vegetarian snack, try to decide on fibre- and protein-rich alternatives, which can assist in stopping endless cravings.

Vegan Recipes

Extraordinary vegetarian plans resemble gold, particularly when they highlight whole foods and heaps of plants. This sort of cooking bolsters your wellbeing and general prosperity in significant ways. No meat? No dairy? No eggs? Try not to sweat it. There are numerous different fixings to get amped up for when you're cooking and eating.

Curried Tomato Tortellini Soup Recipe

Ingredients

- 4 large bunches of spinach, cleaved (or solidified equivalent)
- 2 tablespoons extra virgin olive oil
- 1 medium yellow onion, diced
- 3 cloves garlic, minced

- 2½ teaspoons curry powder
- ¾ teaspoon sweet (or smoked) paprika
- ½ teaspoon ground turmeric
- ¾ teaspoon red chile flakes
- 1 28-ounce can whole tomatoes, with juice
- ¾ cup dried red lentils, flushed
- 4 cups of water
- 1 teaspoon fine grain sea salt, in addition to additional to taste
- 8 ounces (½ pound) crisp tortellini
- To serve: a touch of ground cheddar, lemon (optional)

Instructions

- In case you're using frozen spinach, set it on the counter to defrost.
- Meanwhile, heat the olive oil in an enormous pot over medium-high heat. Mix in the onion and cook, blending infrequently, for 5 minutes or somewhere in the vicinity, until the onion has mollified some. Mix in the garlic, wait a moment, and then add the curry powder, paprika, turmeric, and chili flakes, and mix well.
- Separate the tomatoes with your hands as you add them to the pot along with the tomato juice; mix in the lentils and water. Cover and let cook for 15 minutes or thereabouts, until the lentils have cooked through. Mix in the salt, and afterwards the tortellini. Spread and

cook for another 3-5 minutes or per bundle directions until delicate and cooked through. Mix in the spinach take the consistency back to a stew, and present with dusting of cheddar and a crush of lemon juice. If you have to separate with more water, do as such, and re-season. Enjoy!

Sparkling Cranberries

Ingredients

- ♦ 2 cups cranberries, picked over
- ♦ 2 cups of water
- ♦ 2 cups sugar, plus more for covering

More sugar for covering: I do a blend of medium-grain natural sugar for the main covering, and afterwards a second toss with standard granulated white sugar. You don't need a gigantic grain for that first toss, just an option that is bigger than standard sugar and smaller than most turbinado sugars. You can observe the distinctive grain estimates in the third photograph in the fundamental write-up.

Directions

- ➢ Place the cranberries in a medium glass bowl and put in a safe spot.
- ➢ Make a simple syrup by bringing the water and sugar just to a stew in a medium pot. Let the syrup cool for several minutes, and afterwards pour it over the cranberries. If the syrup is too hot, the cranberries will burst, so be cautious. Cover and refrigerate medium-term.
- ➢ The following day, strain the cranberries and toss them with the bigger grained sugar until they are fully covered. I utilise a scoop of sugar at a time, and little groups of cranberries, so the sugar doesn't get excessively soggy. Spot the covered cranberries on a heating sheet to dry for a couple of hours.
- ➢ Do a second toss with the usual granulated sugar; this ordinarily deals with any clingy spots on the cranberries. Let dry one more hour or somewhere in the vicinity.

The Best Simple Cauliflower Soup

I love the silky surface you get from mixing this soup in a rapid blender, but a B+ level hand-blender functions well also. In this way, don't perspire the equipment side of things to an extreme.

Ingredients

- 2 tablespoons extra virgin olive oil
- 1 huge yellow onion, cleaved
- 3 cloves garlic crushed
- 3 tablespoons yellow curry paste, or more to taste
- 3 little new potatoes, cut into ½-inch 3D shapes
- 1 huge head of cauliflower florets, ~1½ lb.
- 1 teaspoon fine grain sea salt, extra to taste
- ½-1 cup cashew milk or coconut milk
- 1 lime

To serve:

Bread garnishes, or (as pictured) toasted pine nuts, fried shallots, hemp seeds, and a greater amount of the yellow curry paste with a touch of shallot oil.

Directions

- ➢ Empty the olive oil into a huge pot over medium-high heat. When hot, mix in the onion and garlic. Sauté for two or three minutes, sufficiently long for things to mellow. Mix in the curry paste, potatoes, cauliflower, and salt, and permit to cook for an additional 5 minutes or somewhere in the vicinity. Include 4½ cups of water, and heat just to the point of boiling. Dial back the heat and stew sufficiently long for the cauliflower and potatoes to get delicate all throughought, which should be another 5-10 minutes.

➤ Promptly remove the soup from heat, and move to a fast blender (in clusters, if needed). Then again, you can use a hand blender in the pot. Mix in the cashew milk.

➤ Here's the "moment of truth" step — include progressively salt if necessary, and a decent measure of fresh lime juice. Modify until the flavouring is adjusted and without flaw. It should taste brilliant, sharp, and delectable. Serve sprinkled with any/the entirety of the proposed fixings.

Sunshine Pad Thai (Vegetarian)

Rice noodles come in different thicknesses, but I like to choose the wide (¼ inch) ones. To the extent sugar goes, you can use granulated, brown, palm, or coconut sugar here. To go the additional step and make this vegan, you can forget about the egg and it will still be extremely delectable! Keeping things without gluten? Search for tamari or soy sauce.

Ingredients

- 6 ounces dried rice noodles
- ½ tablespoon dried turmeric powder
- 3 tablespoons white vinegar
- 3 tablespoons sugar

- 2 tablespoons vegan "fish" sauce or soy sauce
- 2 tablespoons sunflower oil
- 1 pack of broccolini, cut
- 6 ounces extra-firm tofu, disintegrated
- 1 egg
- ¾ cup bean sprouts or diced celery
- ⅓ cup simmered peanuts
- 3 green onions, thinly sliced
- 2 limes, cut into wedges

Directions

➢ Fill an enormous bowl with simmering water. Mix in the turmeric and the noodles. Use a fork to wash them around a bit, and splash until the noodles are malleable and bendy (5 to 10 minutes). Strain and put in a safe spot.

➢ Meanwhile, whisk together the vinegar, sugar, and soy sauce in a small bowl.

➢ Just before you're prepared to eat, heat the oil in a wok or large skillet over high heat. Mix in the broccoli, spread, and permit to cook for a couple of moments, until the broccolini is splendid green but still somewhat firm. Remove it from the skillet and put in a safe spot.

➢ Next, add the tofu to the skillet, and cook two to three minutes until it starts to turn dark. Add the noodles and the sauce, and mix continually until the noodles assimilate the sauce for a minute or something like that.

➢ Push the noodles to the side, including the egg, whisk, and split it up with the spatula, and enable it to set somewhat (10 or 20 seconds). Split it up, and toss the egg with the noodles. Include the bean sprouts, peanuts, and scallions. Move to a platter and serve with the broccolini and lime wedges.

VIBRANT TASTY GREEN BEANS

The following recipe is best made just before serving time. Rather than cooking the green beans in the skillet, whiten them in a pot of bubbling, well-salted water for about a moment. Strain the beans and dunk them in a bowl of ice water to stop the cooking. Strain and spot the beans again in a pack or bowl in the cooler until prepared to use. When ready, consolidate the components. You can do it at room temperature, or warm them rapidly in a skillet or other container.

Ingredients

- 4 leeks (or 1 pack of scallions), very much washed, root end and tops cut, cut the long way into quarters and afterwards cleaved into 1-inch fragments
- ⅓ cup new dill, all around cleaved
- ¾ pound green beans, tops and tails cut
- Extra-virgin olive oil
- Fine-grain sea salt

Directions:

➤ In an very large thick-bottomed skillet at medium-high heat, include a generous sprinkle of olive oil and a liberal spot of salt on the leeks. Mix until the leeks are covered and gleaming. Cook, blending routinely until most of the leeks is brilliant and firm. I mix each for a moment or two initially, and more frequently as they darken, using a metal spatula. It takes me around 7 to 10 minutes to darken the leeks.

➤ Now mix in the dill, and afterwards mix in the green beans. Cook for a couple more minutes, just until the beans light up and lose that crude chomp. Put into a bowl or onto a platter and serve right away. If you need to set up these green beans early, read the headnotes.

GREAT VEGETARIAN POKE BOWL

Ingredients

- For each bowl:
- ¼ cup cooked short-grain rice
- ⅓ cup watermelon poke
- ½ cup natural tofu, cubed

- ¼ cup lightly cooked asparagus (or another regular vegetable)

Optional toppings:

- Soy sauce, sesame seeds, scallions, daintily cut watermelon radish

Directions

Assemble each poke bowl with the rice as the base. Add in the watermelon, tofu, sprouts, asparagus, and avocado. Finish with a good sprinkle of soy sauce, sesame seeds, scallions, watermelon radish, and more avocado, thinly sliced.

Vegetarian Split Pea Soup

I considered tossing a few bunches of broccolini into this soup a couple of moments before doing the puree, but spinach would be extraordinary also. You can use a vegetable stock if you like instead of the water or bouillon. I at some point use about the portion of one solid form in a soup like this to kick things off — it makes a nice, light broth.

Ingredients

- ◆ 1 tablespoon extra virgin olive oil
- ◆ 2 huge onions, chopped
- ◆ 1 teaspoon fine-grain sea salt
- ◆ 2 cups dried split green peas, picked over and washed

- 5 cups water, in addition to adding more to wrap things up
- Juice of 1 lemon (spare the zest)
- To complete: a couple of portions of smoked paprika, olive oil, toasted almonds, or optionally, scallions

Instructions

➢ Add olive oil to a large pot over medium-high heat. Mix in onions and salt and cook until the onions soften, which takes a moment or two. Include the split peas and water. Heat to the point of boiling, dial down the heat, and stew for 20 minutes, or until the peas are cooked through but still somewhat firm.

➢ Using a large cup or mug, scoop half of the soup into a bowl and put in a safe spot. Using either a hand blender or a normal blender, puree the soup that is still in the pot. Mix the held (still stout) soup once more into the puree, and you ought to have a soup that is pleasantly finished. If you have to thin the soup out with more water (or stock) do such at once — there are times I have to add 3½ cups extra.

➢ Squeeze in the lemon and taste the soup. If it needs more salt, which is likely, include a pinch increasingly until the flavour of the soup truly pops.

Meyer Lemon Focaccia

You essentially need 500g of flour here, and you can mess with various flour blends. Here I use white bread flour, with an addition of (sprouted) rye flour, in addition to a good portion of chopped herbs and hemp seeds. I like this proportion — it brings about focaccia that is generous without being substantial.

Ingredients

- ♦ 3 cups (400 g) solid white bread flour
- ♦ ¾ cup (100 g) rye flour
- ♦ 1 bundle quick-acting instant yeast
- ♦ 1 teaspoon fine grain sea salt

- 1 tablespoon extra virgin olive oil, plus additional for sprinkling
- 3 cloves chopped garlic
- 3 tablespoons hemp seeds (discretionary)
- 2 tablespoons rosemary, finely chopped
- 2 tablespoons thyme, chopped
- ½ cups (350 ml) warm water (~120°F)
- 2 Meyer lemons, cut razor-thin
- 15 dark olives, pitted and split
- ¼ cup sliced almonds

Directions

➢ Consolidate the flours, yeast, salt, olive oil, garlic, hemp seeds, and half of the rosemary and thyme in a huge bowl. Mix in the warm water, and combine until the mixture comes together. Turn out onto a work surface and knead for five minutes or so, until the batter feels smooth and flexible. Rub the batter with a touch of olive oil, and the bowl should be spotless. Cover the bowl with a tea towel and let the dough to rise in a warm, comfortable spot until finished (45 minutes to an hour).

➢ Preheat your stove to 400°F, with the rack in the middle.

➢ You can prepare the focaccia in a container that is 8x12" or larger, or on a free structure on a heating sheet. Tip the batter into the heating container, and empty with level hands. Orchestrate the lemons, olives, and almonds on top, and cover with a tea towel once more. Leave to rise for another 20-30 minutes, until the batter is pleasant and puffy.

➢ Now, use your finger to squeeze openings into the mixture. Sprinkle with extra olive oil and any extra rosemary and thyme. Prepare for thirty minutes, or until brilliant and cooked through. Remove from the oven and cool for a bit before cutting and serving. Sprinkle with more salt if necessary.

Green Falafel Bowl

A few tips: You can use solidified spinach here! Crisp is better, but solidified does work, and you don't need to pre-wash it. To make the falafel vegetarian, you can use flax "eggs" (5 T. water + 2 T. ground flax seeds whisked together), and skip the cheddar. To make it without gluten, use gluten-free oats (beat in a processor) instead of the breadcrumbs. In case you're up for an additional step, roll each ball in prepared breadcrumbs, spritz with olive oil, and pop in the stove. So great!

Ingredients

- ♦ 1 pound (16 ounces) spinach or kale, washed and cut
- ♦ 2 eggs
- ♦ 5 cloves garlic

- 1 cup cooked chickpeas
- 1 cup breadcrumbs
- ½ cup (20 g) ground Parmesan
- 1 teaspoon baking powder
- ¼+ teaspoon fine grain sea salt
- Zest of one lemon

Green Falafel Bowl (pictured):

- 3-4 green falafel, beet hummus, toasted pita wedges, cooked carrots, sliced avocado, & a serving of mixed greens (kale, cucumber, cilantro) all tossed with a sprinkle of olive oil and crush of lemon

Instructions

- ➢ Preheat the broiler to 450°F. Place a large skillet or pot over high heat. When hot, add the spinach, in bunches if necessary. Mix until the greater part of the moisture has dissipated. Move to a cutting board, and cleave well. The more hacked, the better.
- ➢ Consolidate the eggs, garlic, chickpeas, breadcrumbs, cheddar, baking powder, and salt in a blender. Mix until joined. Move to a large bowl, include the lemon zest and chopped spinach, and mix until uniform.
- ➢ With your hands, structure the blend into little ½-inch balls. You should wind up with 20-30 balls. Spot on a baking sheet, smush them down a piece, and put in the broiler for 20 minutes, until toasted, flipping once

along the way. If you don't prepare every one of them, solidify the remaining. You can also cook the falafel in a skillet with a sprinkle of olive oil.

➢ Serve the falafel with a sauce, or with extra segments (recorded in the ingredients list) as a component of a falafel bowl. Enjoy!

QUICK-PICKLED ZUCCHINI

There are a lot of approaches to experiment with the personality of these pickles. In some cases, I shave the zucchini paper-thin, bringing about a wispy tangle of pickled zucchini and onions. On other occasions I need my pickles to have more chomp, structure, and definition. In those cases, I cut the zucchini thicker, maybe ⅛-inch, and let them deplete to the extent that this would be possible, now and then refrigerated.

Additionally, when I make them for our own fixing stash, I use a dark colored common pure sweetener. It gives the pickle fluid an earthy cast that, without exception, weirds people out if they don't have the foggiest idea what is causing it. So in case I'm making the pickles to bring to a barbecue or something, I'll make them with normal natural unadulterated sweetener (one that is lighter in color).

Ingredients

- ♦ 3 medium zucchini (1 pound), thinly cut
- ♦ 1 medium white onion, thinly cut
- ♦ 3 shallots, thinly cut
- ♦ ½ tablespoon fine grain sea salt
- ♦ ¼ cup (small bunch) new dill sprigs
- ♦ 1 little fresh red chili pepper, daintily cut
- ♦ ½ tablespoon yellow mustard seeds
- ♦ ¾ cup cider vinegar
- ♦ ¾ cup white wine vinegar
- ♦ ⅓ cup natural sweetener

Instructions

- ➢ Toss the zucchini, onion, shallots, and salt together in a colander and spot over a bowl to get rid of the fluids. Spread the bowl and refrigerate for anywhere up to a few hours. Toss on more than one along the way. You intend to get as much fluid out of the zucchini as possible. When you're done with the zucchini, shake off any water.
- ➢ Add to a 1 litre/1 quart container alongside the dill, chili pepper, and mustard seeds. I can pack them into a

¾ litre Weck jar, but it's always somewhat cosy in the container.

➢ Consolidate the juices and sugar in a little pan over medium heat. Bring to a stew, mixing until the sugar breaks down, and keep on bubbling for a couple of moments. Pour the fluid over the zucchini and seal the container. Let cool, then refrigerate. The pickles will be good for a week or so.

Simple Sautéed Zucchini Recipe

I prefer not to say this, but if you need bigger amount, double the recipe but partition and cook the zucchini in two dishes. If you group the squash excessively, it steams as opposed to tans and loses a lot of structure, which isn't the thing you're pursuing.

Ingredients

- ♦ 2 tablespoons extra virgin olive oil
- ♦ 5 medium garlic cloves, thinly sliced
- ♦ 3 medium shallots or new red onions, meagerly cut
- ♦ Fine-grain sea salt

- 2 medium zucchini, cut into ¼ inch-thick coins
- A good bunch of dill or potentially scallions, cleaved
- ¼ cup Marcona almonds or toasted almond slices

Instructions

➢ In your biggest skillet, heat the oil over medium-high heat. Mix in the garlic and cook until it begins to take on a trace of shading. Mix in the shallots and a major touch of salt, and cook until they begin to mollify (two or three minutes).

➢ Include the zucchini; mix to get it covered with a bit of oil, and organise the coins in a layer as your skillet allows. Dial the heat up a bit if necessary, include another spot of salt and cook, and mix occasionally until the zucchini browns (ten minutes or thereabouts). Remove from heat and crease in the dill and almonds before serving. Taste, and modify the flavoring if necessary.

An Amazing Vegetarian Paella

Important: Perform a wide search for the perfect paella pan. In a perfect world, this would be 11½ inches in diameter. If you don't have a dish this enormous, or if you don't need leftovers, you may use a 9½-inch container, in which case you need to cut the recipe down the middle (1 cup rice, 2½ cups vegetable stock, ½ cup sofrito, and so forth).

Ingredients

- 3 tablespoons extra virgin olive oil
- 2 spring carrots, ¼-inch dice
- 1 pack of scallions or spring onions, cut into 1-inch pieces
- 3 garlic cloves, chopped

- 2 cups short-grain paella rice
- 1 cup sofrito
- ½ teaspoon smoked paprika
- ½ teaspoon saffron strings
- 3 cups of reduced down blended vegetables: asparagus, peas, cherry tomatoes, summer squash, baby artichokes (cut and quartered), baby radish
- 5 cups hot vegetable stock
- Garnishes: lemon cuts/olives/toasted cut almonds/cleaved herbs

Directions

Beginning

- ➢ Preheat broiler to 300°F. Warmth the olive oil in the skillet.
- ➢ Sauce the carrots and scallions (or spring onions) until translucent. Mix in the garlic and let it cook some more. Include the rice, mix well, and cook until the grains are likewise translucent (a couple of moments). Be careful not to let the rice to overcook. Mix in the sofrito. Include the paprika. Pound the saffron with your fingers, and include that too.

Stew

Mix in the vegetables, pour the hot stock over every last bit of it, mix, and bring to a moderate stew. No more blending permitted. Stew for precisely 17 minutes. Taste the stock and re-season if needed.

Bake the Paella

Move the paella to the broiler and prepare for an additional 12 minutes. Remove if you need to attempt to get more outside on the base of your paella, and you're certain your paella won't burn, return the paella to a burner for one more moment or so. Remove from the heat and enable it to rest for an additional couple of moments. Top with whatever else you like: olives, nuts, lemons, herbs, and so on. Serve family-style in the dish.

BERRY SWIRL ICE CREAM (VEGAN, DAIRY-FREE)

A few things: make the vanilla first, as it commonly takes more time to agitate than organic sorbet. I call for strawberries here, but you can use raspberries, blueberries, blackberries, or a mix! I love the brilliant power of the strawberry, however. Last thing: stir the vanilla and berry in a steady progression; along these lines your dessert should even now be very velvety, enabling you to create a nice swirl. If one of your flavours is excessively solidified, whirling turns out to be additionally challenging.

Ingredients

Vanilla Swirl:

- ♦ 2 cups crude cashews
- ♦ 2 cups of water
- ♦ ½ cup sugar
- ♦ 2 teaspoons vanilla extract
- ♦ ½ vanilla bean
- ♦ ¼ teaspoons salt

Berry Swirl:

- ♦ 12 ounces strawberries, hulled
- ♦ ¼ cup sugar
- ♦ 2 tablespoons lemon juice
- ♦ ⅛ teaspoon salt
- ♦ 1 tablespoon vodka (discretionary)

Directions

Make the vanilla whirl:

Soak the cashews in the water for a couple of hours. Move the cashews, including the water, to a blender. Add the sugar, vanilla extract, vanilla bean, and salt, and puree until rich. Refrigerate until ready to make the ice cream, anywhere up to a couple of days. Agitate in a dessert producer, per the maker's directions. Smear along the inside a cooler or container, and a spot in cooler while you agitate the berry sorbet.

Make the berry twirl:

Puree the berries in a blender. Include the sugar, and mix for one more moment. Include the lemon juice and salt and mix for a couple of more seconds. Strain to dispose of any seeds or pieces. Refrigerate for up to a couple of days, beat per producer's directions, and include the optional vodka close to the end. Move to the compartment with the vanilla, and use a spatula to draw and mix the vanilla through the berry in a few major twirls. Fight the temptation to over-mix.

Grilled Zucchini & Bread Salad

I like multigrain bread here. Tear the bread pieces large enough that the edges get firm, yet the inside remains somewhat chewy. Additionally, if the base of your loaf of bread is extra hard, I would trim that off before adding pieces. Search for ponzu near to the soy sauce at the market.

Ingredients

- ½ pound portion of multi-grain bread, torn into bits
- 2 pounds (4 medium or 2 extra large) zucchini, cut into ¼-inch coins

- ¼ cup extra virgin olive oil
- ⅓ cup ponzu
- 1 tablespoon toasted sesame oil
- 1 medium Serrano pepper, seeded and minced
- 2 cloves garlic, crushed
- 1 14-ounce jar of chickpeas, drained

To serve: zest of one lemon, basil, cherry tomatoes

Instructions

- ➢ Toss the lumps of bread in an enormous bowl with 2 tablespoons of the olive oil and a few pinches of salt. Rub the oil into the bread pieces with your hands, turn out onto a preparing sheet, and toast until well done in a 375°F broiler. It should take 8-12 minutes or something like that, tossing more than once along the way. Put in a safe spot.
- ➢ Whisk the ponzu, toasted sesame oil, Serrano pepper, and garlic together in a little bowl. Put in a safe spot.
- ➢ Prep your broiler at a medium-high warmth. Toss the zucchini in a similar bowl you used for the bread, alongside 2 additional tablespoons of olive oil and 2 or 3 pinches of salt. Either use a wide-flame broiling bin or, if your barbecue has tight braces, spread the zucchini over the grill. Cook for 10-15 minutes, turning regularly with a metal spatula, until the zucchini is delicate and brilliant, with barbecue marks. It may initially appear to be a ton of zucchini, but it really

cooks down. Remove the zucchini from the flame broil as it wraps up.

> Just before serving, pour the ponzu dressing over the flame-broiled zucchini and chickpeas in a huge serving bowl, and gently toss. Include the toasted bread and give another great toss. Serve with cherry tomatoes, lemon zest, and basil.

Sriracha Rainbow Noodle Salad

Appreciate a plate of mixed greens! To make it gluten-free, use rice noodles. You can make the tofu and the dressing early. Try not to hold back on the cilantro!

Ingredients

Sriracha Dressing

- 2 medium cloves garlic, ground
- ⅓ cup sunflower oil
- A couple of drops of toasted sesame oil
- ⅓ cup fresh lime juice

- Liquid sugar (fluid stevia/brown sugar/coconut nectar) to taste
- 1-2 tablespoons Sriracha sauce
- Noodle Salad
- 12 ounces firm tofu, cut into scaled-down pieces
- Toasted
- Fine grain sea salt
- 8 ounces fresh udon noodles, or 4 ounces dried
- 1 teaspoon toasted sesame oil
- ⅔ cup cut scallions/green onion
- 2 cups cilantro leaves and stems, delicately chopped
- A large bunch of shredded basil
- ½ cups finely destroyed cabbage
- 1 cup chopped pineapple (or mango, or peaches!)
- ⅓ cup toasted unsweetened coconut
- ½ cup salted (natural) peanuts
- 3 tablespoons pickled sushi ginger, chopped
- ⅔ cup ground carrots
- 1 medium avocado, sliced
- 3 tablespoons hemp seeds

Directions

Make the Dressing

> Add the garlic, sunflower oil, toasted sesame oil, and lime juice in a container. Add your favored sugar to taste, a little at once, and afterwards add the Sriracha

until it arrives at the ideal measure of spiciness. Put in a safe spot.

Set Up the Tofu

Rub the tofu with a touch of toasted sesame oil and sprinkle with a touch of salt and either flame broil or heat at 350°F until nice and done (ten minutes or somewhere in the vicinity). Put in a safe spot. You can do this as early as a day ahead if you like.

Boil the Noodles

Cook the noodles in a medium pot of salted water. Strain and run under cool water, shaking off any extra, and move to a large serving bowl.

Gather the Noodle Salad

Toss the noodles with the toasted sesame oil and afterwards add the scallions, cilantro, basil, cabbage, pineapple, and the majority of the coconut and peanuts. Pour around two-thirds of the dressing over the top, and give it a good toss. Add the tofu, sushi ginger, carrots, and avocado. Decide if you need any more dressing, and delicately toss once more. Including the carrots at this time prevents them from tinting the remainder of the serving of mixed greens orange. Serve with the rest of the peanuts and coconut, with a liberal sprinkling of hemp seeds.

Roasted Tomato Salsa

The rosy, dark-coloured guajillo pepper is known for its solid, mind-boggling natural flavour, and medium warmth. But if you can't find a guajillo, don't worry. The salsa will still taste delightful with only the cooked tomatoes and chipotles. You can likewise substitute another sort of chili if you like. Don't hesitate to explore different avenues regarding the more easily accessible chilis from your region until you discover one you find best plays off the other kinds of the chipotles and broiled tomatoes. Two chipotles can be hot, so consider yourself warned. Start with one — or even merely a portion of one — chipotle if you or your family are heat-sensitive, and work up from that point.

Ingredients

- 2 pounds Roma tomatoes (or comparable), cut down the middle the long way
- 1 medium white onion, cut into six wedges
- 1 huge garlic clove, divided
- 2-3 pinches of finely ground sea salt
- 2-3 tablespoons of extra-virgin olive oil
- 1 medium dried guajillo chili pepper, oiled until mollified and drained afterwards
- 1-2 chipotles in adobo sauce (canned)
- ½ cup cilantro, chopped

Directions
Broil Ingredients

> Heat stove to 400°F degrees. Delicately toss the tomatoes, onions, garlic, and salt with the olive oil in a large bowl. After they are pleasantly covered, orchestrate in a solitary layer, tomatoes cut-side facing up, over a lined baking sheet. Cook in the stove for 25-30 minutes or until the tomatoes begin to crumble and the onions start to caramelise. Remove from the broiler.

Puree, Chop, and Combine

Puree the chilis (both the guajillo and chipotles) with the cooked garlic and two broiled tomato parts. Cleave the rest of the tomatoes by hand when they've cooled. Cleave and include the onions also. Season with salt liberally, and mix in the cilantro.

Lively Up Yourself Lentil Soup Recipe

I've discovered that French green lentils and dark beluga lentils hold their shape pleasantly; they don't go to mush in the pot. I sometimes use fire-broiled natural crushed tomatoes, and they loan a stunning profound smoky flavour to whatever you use them in. If you come across them, try them out in this soup. If not, standard crushed tomatoes are okay. Likewise, if you can't find Greek yoghurt, just use plain yoghurt. Vegans can avoid the yoghurt totally and finish the soup with a generous drizzle of good olive oil. This recipe makes a huge pot of soup, so I eat the leftovers all week.

Ingredients

- 2 cups dark beluga lentils (or French green lentils), picked over and washed
- 1 tablespoon extra virgin olive oil
- 1 huge onion, sliced
- 1 teaspoon fine-grain sea salt
- 1 28-ounce can crushed tomatoes
- 2 cups water
- 3 cups of a major leafy green (chard, kale, and so forth), washed well, deveined, and finely chopped
- Saffron Yogurt
- A pinch of saffron (30-40 strings)
- 1 tablespoon boiling water
- 2 pinches of salt
- ½ cup 2% Greek yoghurt

Directions

- ➢ Heat 6 cups of water to the point of boiling in an enormous pot, add the lentils, and cook for around 20 minutes, or until delicate. Strain and put in a safe spot.
- ➢ While the lentils are cooking, make the saffron yoghurt by consolidating the saffron strings and boiling water in a small pot. Let the saffron soak for a couple of moments. Presently mix the saffron alongside the fluid into the yoghurt. Blend in the salt and put in a safe spot.
- ➢ In the meantime, heat the oil in a substantial soup pot over medium heat, and add the onion and salt and

sauté until delicate (two or three minutes). Mix in the tomatoes, lentils, and water and keep cooking for a couple of more minutes, letting the soup return up to a stew. Mix in the chopped greens, and wait one more moment. Taste and change the flavouring if need be. Scoop into bowls, and present with a touch of the saffron yoghurt.

Lime & Blistered Peanut Coleslaw

Feel free to forget about the jalapeño if you like it milder. I likewise pondered including crushed, heated tortilla chips (like the ones from the tortilla soup recipe). I've referenced this previously, but I attempt to search out natural peanuts. To the extent that cabbage goes, you can use green cabbage or a mix of purple and green. On the off chance that you like a more velvety coleslaw, feel free to include a bit of mayo or Greek yoghurt!

Ingredients

- ½ cup unsalted crude peanuts
- Half of a medium/large cabbage

- 1 basket of small cherry tomatoes, washed and quartered
- 1 jalapeño pepper, seeded and diced
- ¾ cup cilantro, chopped
- ¼ cup freshly squeezed lime juice
- 2 tablespoons olive oil
- ¼ teaspoon + fine-grain sea salt
- Honey, to taste

Directions

Blister the Peanuts

> In a skillet or stove (350°F), cook the peanuts for 5 to 10 minutes, shaking the dish every once in a while, until golden and blistered.

Set up the Coleslaw Ingredients

Cut the cabbage into two quarters and cut out the centre. Using a knife, shred each quarter into slender cuts. The key here is for them to be reduced down and thin. If any pieces seem as though they may be clumsy, cut those down the middle. Combine the cabbage, tomatoes, jalapeño (optional), and cilantro in a bowl.

Make the Dressing

In a different bowl, toss the lime juice, olive oil, salt. Taste, and add in a teaspoon or two of honey if the lime is too much for you. Add to the cabbage mix and delicately toss. Just before serving, fold in the peanuts (include them too early, and they lose a portion of their crunch). Taste and alter the flavour with salt if necessary.

Avocado Asparagus Tartine

You can cut each tartine into four or five smaller pieces for a pleasant appetizer option also!

Ingredients

- 4-6 toasted pieces of whole grain bread, drizzled with olive oil and a touch of garlic
- ½ tablespoon olive oil
- ½ lb of asparagus stalks, cut around the length of your bread
- 1 clove garlic, finely chopped
- ½ teaspoon caraway seeds
- 1 avocado, pitted and crushed

- Several bunches of arugula, sprinkled with a touch of olive oil
- A bunch of toasted pepitas, almonds, or sunflower seeds
- Lemon zest

Directions

➤ A couple of minutes before you begin eating dinner, heat the olive oil in a large skillet over medium-high heat. When hot, add the asparagus and a touch of salt. Cook for around thirty seconds. Include the garlic and caraway seeds, and cook an additional thirty seconds, or until the spears are a bright green. Remove from heat, and gather together the tartines.

➤ Give each bit of bread a liberal slather of smashed avocado. Top that with a touch of arugula, a couple of asparagus spears, and a liberal sprinkling of pepitas or seeds.

Simple Asparagus Soup

Ingredients

- 2 tablespoons unsalted butter or extra virgin coconut oil
- 1 small onion, chopped
- ½ pound fresh potatoes, cut into small chunks
- 1 tablespoon green curry paste (discretionary)
- 1 pound asparagus, trimmed and cut into ½-inch segments
- 1 14-ounce can full-fat coconut milk
- ½ teaspoon sea salt, to taste
- ¼ cups of water, or enough to cover
- 1 lemon or lime

- To serve: sliced chives, shallots, lemon, and olive oil; or ground hard-boiled egg, herbs, disintegrated whole grain wafers or bread garnishes, crème fraîche

Directions

- In a large soup skillet over medium-high heat, include the spread and onion. Mix until the onion is fully covered, and sauté until translucent. Mix in the potatoes, and cook until totally delicate (around 10 minutes). You can add a sprinkle of water to the dish if it appears to be a touch of moisture will help. Mix in the curry paste, allow it to cook one more moment or two, and afterwards add the coconut milk, salt, and water. Bring to a boil, and add the asparagus. Cook until the asparagus is delicate, 2-3 minutes, and afterwards, puree using a blender or hand blender until the soup is smooth.

- This next part is significant, as with any soup: make any required changes. Include more water if the consistency need be dispersed, a piece after that desire for salt, including more if necessary. I additionally prefer to season this soup with some lemon or lime juice. Serve with whatever you have available. I made it this time around with sliced chives and a shower of shallot oil, but, you can likewise observe an adaptation with ground hard-boiled egg, herbs, wafers, and a touch of crème fraîche. You could sprinkle a couple of chopped almonds on top and call it a day.

Rhubarb & Rosewater Syrup

I use lime here; I think it truly includes something, a required edge. However, lemon is very nice too.

Ingredients

- 4 huge (500 g/1 pound) rhubarb stalks, chopped
- 2 cups granulated sugar
- 2 cups of water
- 2-3 tablespoons freshly pressed lime juice, to taste
- 2 teaspoons rosewater, to taste
- Rose petals (discretionary)

Instructions

- ➤ Combine the rhubarb and sugar in a medium thick-bottomed pan. Mix well, and leave for 45 minutes (unheated), blending once in a while.

- ➤ Add the water and bring to a delicate boil over medium heat, blending until the sugar breaks up. Keep on stewing for another 15-20 minutes, until the rhubarb begins to separate. Cautiously strain into a bowl through a cheesecloth-lined strainer. Move to a perfect pan, mix in the lime juice, and bring to a stew. Let stew over medium heat for an additional 15 minutes or until the syrup has diminished a lot and thickened. Remove from heat and permit it to cool totally.

- ➤ Mix in the rosewater a bit at once, until it is exactly as you would prefer. Rosewater can be a serious emphatic flavour, so be sensitive. It keeps, refrigerated, for a week or somewhere in the vicinity.

- ➤ Serve over yoghurt, in soft drink water, or spread over waffles.

A Few Words on How to Cook Artichokes

On more occasions than not, this is how I like to make artichokes. This method works for whatever artichokes look good at the market, but baby artichokes are perfect. The essence is to trim, blanch, and sauté. You will end up with delightful, delicate, succulent, golden-crusted artichoke hearts that can be appreciated directly from the dish, or in any number of different arrangements. I lay out a couple beneath.

Ingredients

- ♦ Artichokes
- ♦ 1 lemon
- ♦ Extra virgin olive oil or clarified butter

Sea salt

➢ Fill a bowl with water, and crush the juice of the lemon into it. You'll add the artichokes to the water following cutting.

➢ To trim your artichokes: before I dive into the details of cutting, allow me set up the picture of what we're pursuing. We're after a delicate touch. This means we need to trim any extreme external leaves, tips, and stems. We need to get down to the delicate pieces of the leaves, without cutting so much that we only have a minimal amount left. To begin, trim the stem. Force the external leaves from the artichoke, until you get down to the more delicate leaves. To remove the highest point of the artichoke (generally where it starts to decrease in), you need to expel the extreme piece of the tips. I like to use a serrated blade for this cut. From here, choose what shape you'd like your artichoke pieces to be. For this arrangement, I cut every artichoke in equal parts, as well as quarters. If you are using bigger artichokes, ones that have built up a fluffy stifle, you'll have to use a teaspoon (or melon baller) to cut the fluff out before proceeding to your finished products. Work proficiently, and get the cut artichokes in the lemon water as fast as possible to lessen any cooking from oxidation.

➢ While preparing the artichokes, heat a medium pan of water to the point of boiling. Salt well, and use a slotted spoon to move them from the lemon water to the bubbling water. Bubble until simply delicate, which normally takes only a moment or two. Strain well, and put in a safe spot. On the other hand, you can steam the artichokes. This will keep a greater amount of the nutrients unblemished. In any case, you need the artichokes to be cooked delicate (and don't hesitate to eat them now)!

➢ Warm a tablespoon of oil or clarified spread in a large pot over medium-high heat. When hot, move the artichokes to the container in a solitary layer. Cover, and include a squeeze or two of salt. Permit to sauté, tossing at regular intervals, until the artichokes are profoundly brilliant and crusted.

You can enjoy these quickly, or at room temperature, or you can spare them for a couple of days, refrigerated, in a covering of olive oil that you drain before eating.

A couple of different notes:

Buying Artichokes: Your prosperity here will rely upon great sourcing artichokes. Search for tight, thick models. It is an indication that they have been recently collected. If you see that the leaves have begun to bloom out, isolated, or dry out, give them a pass.

Storage: Store artichokes in a pack in your fridge until prepared to use. Attempt to use them rapidly. The sooner, the better.

Adds-ins: This technique makes delightful artichokes in their very own right, but once in a while I like to flare them out with different things I have close by. They have an extraordinary partiality for olives, orange zest, chopped almonds, chili drops, fennel, anise, and lemon oil.

Uses: Once you have a skillet of these, you can eat them all alone, or use them in/on a wide range of things. This artichoke season I've had them on farro risotto, quinoa, frittata, pureed cauliflower soup, and cleaved into ravioli filling. As I'm composing this, I'm envisioning they'd be stunning as a part in a dumpling filling, or spring roll.

The Creamiest Vegan Soup (Cauliflower)

Using a huge 2½- 3 pound head of cauliflower here.

Ingredients

- 2 tablespoons extra virgin olive oil
- ½ yellow onions, chopped
- ½ teaspoon fine grain sea salt, plus extra to taste
- ½ teaspoons ground turmeric
- ½ teaspoons mustard seeds (discretionary)
- 7 cups water; more if necessary
- 1 huge head of cauliflower, cut into florets
- 2 tablespoons dietary yeast

- Black pepper, to taste
- 2 cups yellow split peas, cooked
- Disintegrated kale chips
- Serve with: freshly squeezed lime, dark pepper, squashed bread garnishes, seeds

Directions

- In a thick-bottomed soup skillet, heat the oil over medium heat. Include the onions and salt, and cook for 7 minutes, infrequently mixing, until the onions are translucent. Mix in the turmeric and mustard seeds and cook for another couple of minutes. The mustard seeds may pop, but don't allow them to burn.
- Next, include 2 cups of water, bring to a stew, and mix in the cauliflower. Cover and enable the cauliflower to steam for 10-15 minutes. Include the rest of the water and dietary yeast, and let stew, uncovered, for an additional 5 minutes or so.
- Mix using a hand blender or regular blender. Slim with more water if necessary. Taste and modify with salt and black pepper to taste.
- Serve with a major press of lime, a major scoop of yellow split peas, and some other fixings you like.

How to Make the Creamy, Toasted Coconut Milk of Your Dreams

Make certain to toast your coconut well (but be sure not to burn it!) if you need the flavour to be extra articulated.

Ingredients

- ½ cup toasted coconut
- 4 cups of water
- Fine grain sea or Himalayan salt
- Common sugar, to taste

Directions

- ➤ In a blender, combine the coconut, water, and salt. Blend well.
- ➤ Filter.
- ➤ Improve to taste if you like. I, as a rule, add a couple of drops of fluid stevia, or maple syrup. Refrigerate.

The Ultimate Vegan Nachos

Ingredients

- ◆ 5-6 handfuls of baked tortilla chips
- ◆ 1 can black beans, drained
- ◆ 1 cup sweet potato-based nacho cheddar cheese
- ◆ 1 ripe avocado

Variation #1 toppings (classic):

Any/the entirety of the accompanying: cut olives, cleaved scallions, cilantro, slashed red onions, pickled Serrano chilis*, salsa of your preference

Variety #2 toppings (radical):

Black beans, cooked broccoli, guacamole, cilantro, hemp seeds, pickled Serrano chilis*

Instructions

Preheat broiler to 350°F. Arrange the chips on a baking sheet or platter. Top with the beans and dollops of the cheddar, leaving some extra for later. Heat for ten minutes or somewhere in the vicinity, until the beans and cheddar are warmed through. Meanwhile, in a little bowl, crush the avocado with a fork and a touch of salt. When the chips are warm, remove them from the stove, top with the avocado, and add any other garnishes you like.

Mushroom Scallion Tartine with Poblano Yogurt

To make this dish vegetarian, prepare without dairy yoghurt. To make it gluten-free, substitute a gluten-free bread.

Ingredients

- 12 ounces crisp mushrooms, cut ¼-inch thick
- 3 tablespoons extra virgin olive oil
- Salt and pepper
- 2 bunches of scallions, chopped
- 4 enormous cuts of generous, whole grain bread
- 1 cup Poblano yoghurt*
- 1 cup cooked lentils, or white beans

Directions

- Warmth the broiler to 450°F. Toss the mushrooms with 2 tablespoons of the olive oil and a sprinkling of salt and pepper. Organise in a solitary later on a preparing sheet, spread with aluminium foil (or parchment paper), and heat for around 20 minutes, flipping once en route. Get the scallions in there next. Cut every one of the scallions down the middle the long way, and on a different heating sheet, toss them with the remaining olive oil. Put them in the broiler for around 15 minutes. When each is done, remove, and put in a safe spot. While the mushrooms and scallions are cooking, toast the bread, either in the stove or with a toaster, and if you haven't made the poblano yoghurt* yet, get that ready also.
- To serve, slather each bit of bread with the yoghurt, arrange a couple of mushrooms on top, and finish with the lentils and broiled scallions.

TURMERIC CASHEWS

Ingredients

- ♦ 2 cups raw cashews
- ♦ ½ tablespoon toasted sesame oil, or to taste
- ♦ ¼ teaspoon fine grain ocean salt, or to taste
- ♦ 8x8-inch sheet nori
- ♦ ½ teaspoons sesame seeds
- ♦ ¼ teaspoon cayenne
- ♦ ½ tablespoon ground turmeric

Directions

- ➢ Toss the cashews with the sesame oil and sea salt and toast in a 350°F stove for 5-10 minutes, or until done, tossing once en route. Remove and toast the kelp for a couple of moments. Let it cool, and then shred it.

➢ Consolidate the kelp, sesame seeds, and cayenne in a mortar and pestle, and crush together. In a bowl (one that won't recolor), hurl the cashews with the sesame flavours and turmeric. Truly pull out all the stops. If you have to include a couple of drops of sesame oil, do as such to saturate things up a bit. Taste and alter the seasonings, if need be.

A California Panzanella

Ingredients

- ◆ 2 thick cuts of healthy multi-grain bread
- ◆ 2 tablespoons extra-virgin olive oil
- ◆ Fine-grain sea salt
- ◆ 12-ounce block extra-firm tofu, cut into 4 slabs
- ◆ ⅓ cup all-natural nut spread
- ◆ 2 tablespoons brown rice or apple juice vinegar
- ◆ 1 clove garlic
- ◆ ½ teaspoon toasted sesame oil
- ◆ ¼ teaspoon red pepper flakes
- ◆ ⅓-⅔ cup hot water

- ♦ 1½ cups sprouts
- ♦ ½ cup stove cooked or sun-dried tomatoes

Directions

- ➢ Warm the stove to 375°F. Cut the bread into 1-inch solid chunks, and toss with the olive oil and a liberal sprinkling of salt. Prepare until brilliant and crunchy (ten minutes or somewhere in the vicinity).
- ➢ Brush the tofu with a touch of extra virgin olive oil. Place it on a sheet dish and heat, flipping once, until done on the two sides (7 minutes or somewhere so on each side). Remove from the broiler, cut into ½-inch pieces, and place in a large bowl.
- ➢ Meanwhile, make the nut dressing by consolidating the nut spread, vinegar, garlic, sesame oil, red pepper pieces, and ¼ teaspoon of salt into a medium bowl. Meagre with the hot water. I like the dressing to be the consistency of flimsy, dissolved frozen yoghurt. Taste and modify with salt or pepper drops, if necessary.
- ➢ Just before serving, pour a liberal measure of the dressing over the tofu, and toss it tenderly. It should look much overdressed now. Include the bread and delicately toss once more. Turn out onto a platter and top with the sprouts and afterwards the tomatoes. Serve at room temperature.

Make-Ahead Vegan Samosa Shepherd's Pie

Cold-weather comfort food, without a great deal of the trappings. You can make the "covering" with sweet potatoes, potatoes, or a mix of the two. You can get ready early and prepare just before serving. If you use sweet potatoes, skin them.

Ingredients

- ½ pound potatoes or sweet potatoes
- ⅔ cup full-fat coconut milk
- Fine grain sea salt, to taste
- 1 tablespoon coconut oil
- 1 medium onion, sliced

- 4 cloves garlic, minced
- 8 ounces mushrooms, cut
- 1 cup crushed tomatoes
- 2 teaspoons garam masala
- 2 cups cooked yellow or green split peas
- 1 cup peas (crisp or solidified)

To serve: Add a sprinkle of liquefied coconut oil with cut Serrano chilis, smaller-scale greens, and scallions.

Directions

- Preheat broiler to 375°F with the rack in the middle.
- Put the potatoes/sweet potatoes in a medium pan, spread with water, and salt as you would pasta water. Heat to the point of boiling for around ten minutes, or until delicate. Strain, and add them back to the pan over heat for a moment or so to dry them out. Include the coconut milk and the salt, and crush together. Put in a safe spot.
- In a large pot over medium-high heat, consolidate the coconut oil with the onion, garlic, and a liberal spot of salt. Sauté for a couple of moments, until onions are translucent, and afterwards turn the heat up and add the mushrooms. Cook, mixing every couple of minutes, until the mushrooms discharge their water, and begin to darken. Add the tomatoes and zests. Mix well, and at that point include the cooked peas. Cook for one

more moment or two, taste, and alter with more garam masala or salt if necessary.

➢ Move the mushroom blend to an 8-inch heating dish (or equivalent), spreading it crosswise over in a fairly even layer. Put the potatoes over the top, and delicately move them around until they spread the whole top of the goulash.

➢ Prepare for 25 minutes, and finish in the warming tray under the oven to include a touch of additional shading and surface to the top. Fill in as need be, or sprinkle with any or all of the recommended fixings.

This is How You Step Up Your Guacamole Game

Ingredients

- ♦ 2 ripe avocados
- ♦ 2 teaspoons new lemon juice
- ♦ ½ teaspoon fine-grain sea salt
- ♦ ½ cup coarsely cleaved crisp cilantro
- ♦ 1 tablespoon clarified spread or extra virgin coconut oil
- ♦ 1 teaspoon black or brown mustard seeds
- ♦ 1 small yellow onion, minced
- ♦ 2 cloves garlic, finely cleaved
- ♦ 1 teaspoon curry powder
- ♦ 1 small Serrano chili, minced

Directions

➢ Cut each avocado down the middle, remove the pit, and scoop the fruit into a little bowl. Include the lemon juice, salt, and a greater part of the cilantro. Crush the avocados with a fork a bit, but not too much — you need the blend to be very stout. Put in a safe spot.

➢ Warmth the clarified spread or oil in a skillet over medium-high heat. When it is hot, include the mustard seeds. Keep a close eye because the seeds will disperse as they pop. When the splashing stops, after about a moment, mix in the onion and sauté for 2 to 3 minutes until the onion is translucent. Mix in the garlic, curry powder, and chili. Count to ten, and then remove from heat. Mix in the avocado blend and move to a serving bowl. Serve warm or at room temperature. Enhancement with any leftover cilantro.

Magic Sauce

Ingredients

- ½ cup extra virgin olive oil
- 1 teaspoon crisp rosemary leaves
- 1 teaspoon crisp thyme leaves
- 1 teaspoon crisp oregano leaves
- 2 teaspoons sweet paprika
- 2 medium cloves of garlic, crushed into a paste
- 1 well-disintegrated bay leaf
- Spot of red pepper chips
- ¼+ teaspoon fine grain sea salt
- 1 tablespoon crisp lemon juice

Directions

➤ Tenderly warm the olive oil over medium-low heat in a skillet or dish, until it is hot. Remove from heat.

➤ While the oil is warming, gently pound the rosemary, thyme, and oregano using a mortar and pestle.

➤ Mix the paprika, garlic, bay leaf, red pepper pieces, and salt into the oil. At that point, include the crushed herbs and lemon juice.

➤ You can use this right away, but know that the oil will show signs of improvement as it ages over a couple of days. Keep it in a cooler for as long as 7-10 days. It thickens up when cold, so if you need it in a fluid state, place it in the sun or a warm spot for a couple of moments.

Simple Brown Rice Sushi Bowl

Ingredients

- ♦ 2 4-inch square sheets of nori seaweed
- ♦ 6 ounces extra-firm tofu
- ♦ Ground zest and the juice of one orange
- ♦ Ground zest and the juice of half a lemon
- ♦ 2 tablespoons (crude) brown sugar (regular sugar is alright as well)
- ♦ 2 tablespoons shoyu sauce (or soy sauce)
- ♦ 2 tablespoons (brown) rice vinegar
- ♦ 4 cups cooked brown rice, warm
- ♦ 4 green onions, chopped
- ♦ 1 avocado, stripped, pitted, and thinly cut
- ♦ 3 tablespoons sesame seeds, toasted

Directions

➢ Toast the nori in a preheated 300°F degree broiler or a medium-hot skillet for a couple of moments. Disintegrate or chop coarsely.

➢ Strain the tofu and pat it dry. Cut the square of tofu the long way through the centre to make four ¼- to ½-inch thick sheets of tofu. Cook two at once in a dry skillet or well-prepared skillet over medium-high heat for a couple of moments until sautéed on one side. Flip tenderly; at that point, keep cooking for one more moment or thereabouts, until the tofu is firm. Rehash with the rest of the sheets.

➢ To make the dressing, put the sheets in a safe spot. Consolidate the squeezed orange and lemon juices and sugar in a little pan and bring to a delicate bubble. Cook for 1 or 2 moments, then add the shoyu and vinegar.

➢ Bring back to a delicate boil and cook another 1 or 2 minutes, until marginally thickened. Remove from the heat and mix in the zest.

➢ Mix in ⅓ cup of the dressing into the rice and add more to taste. Scoop the rice into dishes and top each with the toasted nori, green onions, tofu, avocado slices, and a sprinkling of sesame seeds.

Orange Pan-Glazed Tempeh

This recipe can also be made with tofu. I made a couple of minor changes to the recipe according to American ingredients/estimations. You can make a dinner out of this by blending it with some gently sautéed seasonal vegetables, though this situation, I just served it over some left-over cooked wheat berries that I warmed with a touch of chopped kale.

Ingredients

- 1 cup freshly pressed orange juice (requires 3-4 large oranges)
- 1 tablespoon freshly ground ginger
- 2 teaspoons tamari (or soy sauce)

- ½ tablespoons mirin
- 2 teaspoons maple syrup
- ½ teaspoon ground coriander
- 2 little garlic cloves, crushed
- 10 ounces of tempeh (or extra-firm tofu)
- 2 tablespoons coconut oil, ghee, or olive oil
- ½ lime
- A bunch of cilantro (coriander) leaves

Directions

> Put the squeezed orange juice in a little bowl. Press the ground ginger over the bowl to separate the juices, then dispose of the mash. Include the tamari, mirin, and maple syrup, ground coriander, and garlic. Combine and put in a safe spot.

> Cut the tempeh (or tofu) into slices, reduced down pieces, and if working with tofu, pat dry with a paper towel.

> Put the coconut oil in a large skillet over medium-high heat. When the oil is hot but not yet smoking, add the tempeh and fry for 5 minutes, or until done underneath. Turn and cook the opposite side for an additional 5 minutes, or until done. Empty the squeezed orange blend into the skillet and stew for 10 minutes, or until the sauce has decreased to a dazzling thick coating. Turn the tempeh again during this time and spoon the sauce over the tofu now and again. Serve

the tempeh showered with any leftover sauce and a crush of lime, with the coriander dissipated on top.

Make-Ahead Super Green Vegan Quinoa Burritos

Don't hesitate to replace the wrap itself if tortillas aren't your thing — collard leaves, kale, or sheets of nori are other choices.

Ingredients

- ♦ 1 avocado
- ♦ 2 cloves garlic
- ♦ 4 scallion, cut
- ♦ A bunch of chives, basil, or potentially cilantro
- ♦ ¼ cup tahini or almond butter
- ♦ ¼ cup water
- ♦ 5 tablespoons lemon juice

- Salt or coconut aminos, to taste
- 1 Serrano chili pepper (discretionary)
- 2 bunches of kale, de-stemmed, and cut
- 6 multi-grain or spinach tortillas
- 3 cups cooked mung beans
- 3 cups cooked quinoa
- Optional: toasted pepitas, hemp seeds

Directions

> Consolidate the avocado, garlic, scallion, herbs, tahini, water, lemon juice, salt, and chili in a blender or processor and mix until smooth. Move to a container.

> Put the kale in a huge bowl, and include around half of the dressing to it. Rub with your hands until the kale is pleasantly covered and starting to crumple a bit.

> Place one tortilla on the counter and load up with around ½ cup of the quinoa, ½ cup of the mung beans, a couple of liberal dabs of the dressing, a bunch of the kale blend, and a sprinkling of pepitas and hemp seeds (if desired). Crease and roll, and afterwards rehash with the remaining tortillas. Enclose each with parchment paper, and afterwards foil in case you're anticipating eating later.

Broccoli Cheddar Soup

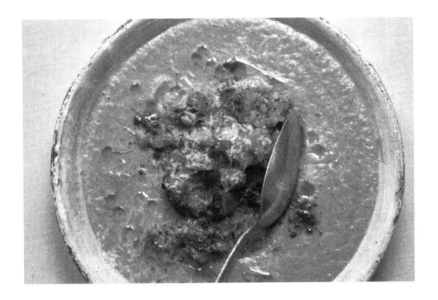

Search for bright green, tight heads of broccoli. I ordinarily maintain a strategic distance from any heads that have yellowing florets or appear to have missing florets. If you like a creamier soup, mix in a liberal dab of crème fraîche in the wake of pureeing. You can without much of a stretch make this soup vegan by using olive oil and precluding the cheddar or crème fraîche, and you can make it gluten-free by abstaining from the bread garnishes.

Ingredients

- croutons
- 5-6 ounce chunk of artisan whole wheat bread, cut into little pieces (under 1-inch) (approximately 3 cups total)

98

- ¼ cup softened margarine or olive oil (I like 1/2 and 1/2)
- ½ tablespoons whole grain mustard
- ¼ teaspoon fine grain sea salt

Soup:

- 2 tablespoons unsalted margarine or olive oil
- 1 shallot, sliced
- 1 medium onion, sliced
- 1 large potato, stripped and cut into ¼-inch blocks (½ cups)
- 2 cloves garlic, finely chopped
- 3½ cups light vegetable stock
- 12 ounces or ¾ lb. broccoli, cut into little florets
- ⅔ cup freshly shredded matured cheddar, plus extra for garnish
- 1-3 teaspoons whole grain mustard, to taste
- Optional: smoked paprika, olive oil, crème fraîche

Directions

➢ Preheat your broiler to 350°F and put the torn bread in an large bowl. In a small pot, heat the margarine until it has liquefied. Whisk the mustard and salt into the margarine and pour the blend over the bread. Toss well, then turn the bread onto a heating sheet and prepare for 10-15 minutes, or until the bread garnishes are brilliant and crunchy. Toss them a few times with a metal spatula along the way.

➢ While the bread garnishes are toasting, soften the margarine or olive oil in a large pan over medium-high heat. Mix in the shallots, onion, and a major touch of salt. Sauté for 2-3 minutes. Mix in the potatoes, spread, and cook for around 4 minutes, or sufficiently long for them to mollify. Remove; mix in the garlic and the soup. Heat to the point of boiling, taste to ensure the potatoes are delicate, and if they are, mix in the broccoli. Stew sufficiently long for the broccoli to get delicate all through, 2-4 minutes.

➢ Promptly remove the soup from the heat and puree with a submersion blender. Include a large portion of the cheddar and the mustard. On the off chance that you are going to include any crème fraîche, this would be an ideal opportunity to do it. Presently include more water or stock if you want to disperse the soup any. Taste and add salt if necessary.

➢ Serve sprinkled with croutons, the rest of the cheddar, a shower of olive oil, and a modest touch of smoked paprika.

Golden-Crusted Sesame-Seeded Tofu

Ingredients

- ◆ 12 ounces extra-firm tofu, strained and pat dry
- ◆ 2 tablespoons soy sauce or coconut aminos
- ◆ 4 tablespoons sesame seeds
- ◆ ½ tablespoon extra virgin olive oil

Directions

➤ Pat the tofu dry and cut it into ½-inch by 1-inch sticks. Tenderly hurl the tofu with the soy sauce, and permit to sit for 2-3 minutes. Pour the seeds onto a plate. Get a tofu rod, dunk one side into the seeds, and move to another plate. Repeat with all the tofu sticks.

- ➤ This is one of only a handful of situations in which I want to use a non-stick container. Then again, a very well-seasoned cast iron dish will also work. Warm the oil over medium-high heat, and arrange the tofu, seeded side down, in the skillet. Cook until done on the bottoms, 4-5 minutes. Darken the rest of the sides, and remove from skillet. Fill in as need be, or as envisioned (over fire-broiled green beans), to finish off a rice bowl, or over whatever broiled vegetables you may have!

WEEKNIGHT PONZU PASTA

I've been getting a kick out of this chickpea pasta as of late (produced using chickpea flour). It's pleasant supposing that you're serving a group, as it is gluten-free. On the ponzu sauce front, I prefer the "From Japan" brand natural ponzu, but there are a decent number of vegan ponzu alternatives out there. Pick one that you prefer; ideally organic, without an excessive amount of salt. A tip on this: avoid the pasta, and swap in a container of garbanzo beans (flushed, strained). Or then again, exchange out the tofu for chickpeas. If you need to make this in a hurry, for a gathering or cookout later, run every fixing under cool water to stop the cooking, and combine just before serving.

Ingredients

- 8 ounces additional firm tofu, cut into ¼-inch solid shapes
- 8 ounces small pasta
- 6 tablespoons ponzu sauce
- 3 garlic cloves, minced
- ½ teaspoon chile drops, or to taste
- ¼ teaspoon toasted sesame oil
- 8 ounces green beans, cleaved
- 8 ounces broccoli florets
- A small bundle of cilantro (or basil), chopped
- Optional: cherry tomatoes, hemp hearts, disintegrated kale chips, makrut lime

Directions

- To make the dressing, in a small bowl whisk together the ponzu, garlic, chili, and sesame oil. Taste, modify, and put in a safe spot.
- When the pasta water is boiling, salt the water, add the pasta, and cook per guidelines. Use a strainer to move the cooked pasta into a serving bowl. Use the still-boiling pasta water to cook the green beans for a moment, add the broccoli, and allow to cook one more moment until both are delicate. Rapidly strain and move to the bowl with the pasta.

➤ Include the tofu and the ponzu dressing, and toss well. Add the cilantro and some other extra fixings, give one final toss, and serve right away.

An Immunity Soup to Light up Your Insides

Modify the broth regularly — if it's summer, toss some corn in. Spring? Go for cut asparagus. Additionally, for a more generous meal, serve over brown rice or soba noodles. Delicious! A mandolin makes snappy work of all the cutting here, but watch those fingers! I like enoki or nameko mushrooms. Black trumpets are great, and normal brown mushrooms do the job too.

Ingredients

- 1 tablespoon extra virgin olive oil
- 1 medium onion, quartered and daintily cut
- 3 celery stalks, daintily cut

- 1 medium carrot, daintily cut
- 8 medium garlic cloves, daintily cut
- 2 tablespoons ground ginger, stripped
- ¾ teaspoon finely ground white pepper, plus extra to taste
- ½ cups mushrooms, cut
- 8 ounces firm tofu, cut into dainty chunks
- 2½ teaspoons fine grain sea salt

To serve: heaps of slashed green onions, cut watermelon radish, and pea shoots

Instructions

> Warm the oil in a large soup pot over medium heat. Mix in the onion, celery, carrot, garlic, and ginger. Delicately sauté just until delicate — you don't need any caramelizing. Include a little sprinkle of water if the skillet is dries out.

> Mix in the white pepper and 10 cups of water. Dial up the heat to bring the juices to a boil, and hold there for around 15 minutes. Add the mushrooms, tofu, and salt, and gently boil for an additional 5 minutes. Mix well, taste, and change with salt or water if necessary. Spoon the soup into shallow soup bowls and top with heaps of green onions, pea shoots, and a couple of watermelon radish cuts. Include a finishing sprinkle of olive oil, and enjoy!

A Glow-Promoting, Luminizing Breakfast Beauty Bowl

If you don't have a couple of the topping ingredients, it's no biggie. Start with the smoothie base and work from that point, concentrating on what is seasonal, fresh, and accessible in your area.

Ingredients

- ♦ 1 cup frozen, naturally blended berries (blueberries, strawberries, blackberries)
- ♦ 1 teaspoon chia seeds
- ♦ ½ cup unsweetened yoghurt or nut milk

- Liquid sugar, to taste (coconut nectar, liquid stevia, maple syrup)

Toppings: pineapple wedges, citrus slices, pomegranate seeds (and juice), granola or toasted oats, dried berries (whole and crushed), honeybee dust, cacao nibs, toasted coconut, slashed nuts

Directions

- Mix the berries, chia seeds, and yoghurt or nut milk until smooth. Improve as you would prefer, and move to a serving bowl (or split between two serving bowls).
- Place a couple of pineapple wedges and citrus fragments in each bowl and give a fast toss. Sprinkle with pomegranate seeds, granola, toasted coconut, and any of different garnishes you like and have available.

Ribollita, the Tuscan Stew You Should Be Eating Regularly

In regards to the choice of beans, I as a rule select cannellini. On the bread front, I regularly use a portion of day-old whole wheat sourdough, though I have on occasion opted for crusty bread. Canned beans can be used here, and the proportion is approximately a few 15-ounce jars. To the extent that kale goes, search for cavolo nero, a rocky evergreen-hued kale that may also be marked as lacinato or Tuscan kale. The ribollita is imagined here showered with a simple herb oil made by pureeing olive oil, a couple of garlic cloves, parsley, and marjoram together.

Ingredients

- 3 tablespoons extra virgin olive oil, plus additional for sprinkling
- 4 celery stalks, cleaved
- 3 medium cloves garlic, cleaved
- 2 medium carrots or equivalent amount of winter squash, cleaved
- 1 medium red onion, cleaved
- 1 14-ounce (400 ml) can crushed tomatoes
- ½ teaspoon crushed red pepper pieces
- 1 pound (16 ounces or 450 g) cavolo nero/lacinato kale/Tuscan kale, stems cut off and leaves very much slashed
- 4 cups (22 oz) cooked white beans
- ½ pound (8 oz) crustless part of bread
- ½+ teaspoon fine grain sea salt
- Zest of one lemon
- Heaps of well-slashed oily black olives

Instructions

➢ In your largest thick-bottomed pot over medium heat, consolidate the olive oil, celery, garlic, carrot, and red onion. Cook for 10-15 minutes, sweating the vegetables yet keeping them away from any caramelizing. Mix in the tomatoes and red pepper pieces, and stew for an additional 10 minutes or thereabouts, long enough for the tomatoes to thicken up a piece. Mix in the cavolo nero, 3 cups of the beans, and 8 cups water. Heat to the point of boiling, turn down the heat, and stew until the greens are delicate (around 15 minutes).

➤ Meanwhile, pound or puree the rest of the beans with a liberal sprinkle of water until smooth. Tear the bread into chunks. Mix both the beans and bread into the soup. Stew, blending at times, until the bread separates and the soup thickens (20 minutes or something like that). Mix in the salt, taste, and include more if necessary. Mix in the lemon zest.

➤ Serve quickly, or cool and refrigerate medium-term. Serve warm or "ribollita," which means reboiled, the following day scooped into bowls. Finish each with a drizzle of olive oil and some cleaved olives.

LAST-MINUTE RED LASAGNA

I've used all of the following types of noodles at some point with this recipe: new egg pasta, new spinach pasta, new whole wheat pasta, and dried, no-boil whole wheat pasta (something like this). All work extraordinary! Likewise, I regularly make a vegetarian adaptation in which I skirt the mozzarella inside and out. Rather, flimsy out certain tahini with warm water, season with salt and garlic paste, and use that as a rich completing shower. If you like a cheesier lasagna, you can unquestionably include some ricotta in substituting layers! This is excessively simple to adjust.

Ingredients

- 28-ounce container of crushed tomatoes

- 2 tablespoons extra virgin olive oil
- ½ teaspoon fine grain salt
- 2 cloves garlic, cleaved
- ½ teaspoon red pepper pieces
- lemon zest
- 12 ounces new pasta sheets, cut into lasagna strips OR 9 ounces dried entire wheat no-bubble lasagna sheets
- 1 cup cooked red lentils or cannellini beans
- ¼ cup cleaved olives (discretionary)
- 4 ounces mozzarella cheddar, torn

Directions

Preheat the stove to 400°F with a rack in the top third of the oven.

Assemble the Lasagna

> To assemble the lasagna, consolidate the tomatoes, olive oil, salt, garlic, and red pepper drops in a bowl and give it all a good mix.

> Spoon ¾ cup of the sauce into the base of a 8x12-inch (or bigger) dish. Sprinkle liberally with lemon zest, and spread with a layer of pasta, giving the pasta strips a fast dunk in cool water before placing. Kindly observe the note below if using no-bubble noodles*.

> Spoon another slim layer of tomato sauce, sprinkle with a couple of tablespoons of the lentils, place the olives (if using), and spread with another layer of

pasta. Rehash with more layers, spreading a liberal measure of tomato sauce on top. Finish with the mozzarella cheddar on top (or see headnotes for vegetarian rendition).

Heat

Bake for 30 minutes, or until the cheddar gets pleasantly browned.

CAP BEAUTY NO-BONE BROTH

If you'd like juice that runs more salty, use dried shiitake mushrooms. Likewise, your soups and stocks are just in the same class as your water. Use extraordinary-tasting water here — filtered water is best. Something you would mix a good tea in.

Ingredients

- 3 (2-inch) bits of kombu
- 8 cups of water
- 1 yellow onion, slashed
- 1 tablespoon olive oil
- 1 carrot, slashed (1 cup)
- 1 leek, slashed (1 cup)
- ½ cup dried porcini, chanterelle, or shiitake mushrooms (or a mix)
- 1 (2-inch) bit of ginger, chopped
- 1 (2-inch) bit of turmeric, chopped
- 1 head garlic, unpeeled, divided transversely
- 1-2 tablespoons dried, shredded wakame or dulse
- 6 sprigs of thyme
- 2 bay leaves
- 1 teaspoon black peppercorns
- 2-3 dried red chilis

Directions

➤ Soak the kombu in 4 cups of water for as long as 4 hours. In an large stockpot, sauté the onions in the olive oil until they become translucent. Add the carrot and leek. Keep sautéing for 8-10 minutes, or until the vegetables mollify.

➤ Add the kombu and its water to the pot. Pour in the remaining 4 cups of water, and add the mushrooms, ginger, turmeric, garlic, wakame, thyme, bay leaves, peppercorns, and chilis. Warm over medium heat. Right before the pot boils, take out the kombu and dispose of it. Let the rest of the stock boil and reduce to a stew. Delicately cook for 2 hours.

➢ Strain the stock carefully through a fine strainer. Dispose of the vegetables, or put them aside for another recipe. Taste the juices and include salt, lemon or lime juice, vinegar, or your choice of oil to taste.

GOLDEN BEET HUMMUS

You can make this with raw or broiled beets! The beets envisioned in this rendition were raw. What's more, you can use red or purple beets. If you find turmeric excessively harsh or unpleasant/tannic, start with less, and include more to taste. I require a scope of flavours/additional items — turmeric, saffron, and dietary yeast. All give some wholesome lift to this hummus, but you can surely forget about them if you don't have them already. The stunning shading here gets more from the turmeric versus the beets, so remember that. My primary proposal is to make a triple cluster to keep close by all week.

Ingredients

- 1 14-ounce can chickpeas, drained and washed
- 1 medium brilliant beet (crude), stripped, and quartered (4-inch measurement)
- 4-6 tablespoons fresh lemon juice (2 lemons)
- 4 medium garlic cloves
- ¼ teaspoon fine grain sea salt, plus additional to taste
- 2 tablespoons tahini
- ⅓-½ cup ice water
- ¾ teaspoon ground turmeric (discretionary)
- Touch of saffron (discretionary)
- 3 tablespoons dietary yeast (discretionary)
- To serve (all or a portion of the others): sesame seeds, hemp seeds, edible flowers, cleaved chives, toasted sesame oil

Directions

- Strip the chickpeas by popping each one out of its skin. This will make your hummus smoother. If you can't stand the possibility of this (reasonable!), avoid this step. Your hummus won't be as smooth, but it will still be as scrumptious.
- Put the chickpeas into a blender or food processor and puree into a thick paste. Add the beets and puree once more. Then add the lemon juice, garlic, salt, and tahini. Gradually sprinkle in the cold water. Continue preparing for a couple of minutes (3 or somewhere in

120

the vicinity). Include the turmeric, saffron, and dietary yeast, and give another turn. Taste and modify with salt or lemon juice if necessary. This recipe calls for significantly less salt than numerous other hummus recipes, the thought being that you start with the most minimal amount and afterwards adding it to taste.

➤ Smear the hummus over a serving plate or bowl, and top with any of the proposed fixings.

INSTANT POT MUSHROOM STROGANOFF WITH VODKA

If your mushrooms look grimy or dusty, wipe them with a damp fabric or paper towel. I used chickpea pasta here, and it works incredibly! If vodka is badly designed, substitute a another spirit (whiskey was tasty), or white wine.

Ingredients

- 1 teaspoon caraway seeds, crushed
- ⅓ cup vodka
- 1 tablespoon extra virgin olive oil
- 1 medium yellow onion, chopped
- 3 garlic cloves, stripped and chopped

- 1 pound dark-coloured mushrooms, stemmed and slashed to ½-inch
- 2 tablespoons tomato paste
- 1 tablespoon flour
- 2 tablespoons Dijon mustard
- ¾ teaspoon fine grain sea salt, plus additional to taste
- ¼-½ teaspoon newly ground pepper, or to taste
- 1¾ cup mushroom soup (or vegetable stock)
- 2 cups dried pasta (see headnotes)
- ½ cup handcrafted cashew cream* or almond milk

To serve: bunches of dill or chives, toasted almonds

Directions

> In a small bowl, consolidate the caraway seeds and the vodka, then put in a safe spot. Sauté the olive oil and onions in the Instant Pot on the highest saute setting for a moment or two. Mix in the garlic and mushrooms, and cook for a couple of moments more until everything relaxes. Mix in the tomato paste and afterwards the flour, and cook, blending tenderly yet continually for an additional couple of moments, to toast the flour. Include the mustard, salt, and pepper, soup, and pasta. Give one final stir to disperse the pasta uniformly, and press cancel to stop the saute.

> Close the pot and secure the cover. seal the valve. Select pressure cook (or manual) and figure your cooking time. To do this, refer to your pasta box; the time will

be half of the briefest prescribed cooking time, adjusted down to the closest moment. For instance, my pasta box prescribed 7-9 minutes. Take the more modest number (7), cut down the middle (3.5), and round down to closest entire number (3). set/adjust time. In my situation, this would be 3 minutes. At the point when completed, cautiously quick release pressure by moving the valve to venting. Delicately shake or tap the pressure cooker, and afterwards, cautiously open away from you.

➢ Mix in the vodka-caraway blend, stew for a couple of more minutes, and mix in cashew milk. Taste and alter flavoring, then serve topped with heaps of dill and almonds.

Quick Vegan Enchiladas with Sweet Potato Sauce

Two or three hints: you need to use adaptable, flexible tortillas at room temperature or hotter. In case your tortillas are on the solid side, place them in a baking dish, covered, in a warm stove for a couple of moments to mollify. Or on the other hand, if you have a microwave, give them a snappy hit. Play around with fillings here — a limited quantity of crumbled feta (in case you're not vegan) or plant-based equivalent, included alongside the black beans, adds a good velvety touch to the filling — a pleasant highlight without fighting be the headliner. ;)

Ingredients

- 1 tablespoon extra virgin olive oil
- 1 15-ounce can sweet potato puree, butternut squash puree, or pumpkin puree
- ½ teaspoon turmeric powder
- 2 medium cloves garlic
- 1 tablespoon taco seasoning
- ¾ teaspoon fine grain sea salt
- 1 lemon, zest and juice
- 8 corn tortillas (6-inch), room temperature or warm
- 1 15-ounce can black beans, strained and flushed
- ⅓ cup slashed black olives
- ⅓ cup tahini
- ½ cup cut almonds
- ½ cups slashed cilantro leaves

To serve: broiler-cooked tomatoes, Serrano vinegar and chilis*, a preferred salsa, and so forth.

Directions

Preheat stove to 425°F.

Make the Filling

In a large bowl, combine the olive oil, sweet potato puree, turmeric, half of the ground garlic, taco seasoning, salt, zest of the lemon, and ½ cups of water. Mix well.

Collect the Enchiladas

Scoop a cup of the sweet potato blend into the base of an 8x12-inch or bigger heating dish. Lay the tortillas on a work surface, and gap the black beans similarly between them. Sprinkle similarly with olives. Move the tortillas, and place crease-side down in the heating dish. Pour the rest of the sauce on top. It will thicken.

Prepare and Make Sauce

Prepare the enchiladas for 30-35 minutes or thereabouts. Part of the way through, sprinkle with sliced almonds, and complete the process of preparing until brown and bubbling. While the enchiladas are cooking, slim the tahini with ¼ cup warm water. Add in the rest of the garlic, a touch of salt, and crush of lemon juice. Top the enchiladas with bits of the tahini sauce and the crisp cilantro when they leave the stove. Serve hot!

WHITE BEAN SOUP WITH PESTO HERB DUMPLINGS

To make this soup vegan, skip the egg in the dumpling and knock the almond milk up to ¼ cup. The dumplings won't be as delicate, but they will still be great. I additionally prefer to make this soup with a mustard garnish or (!) a harissa highlight in the dumplings. For this, discard the pesto, and use either 1 tablespoon Dijon-style mustard or 2 tablespoons harissa paste.

Ingredients

White Bean Soup

- ◆ 1 huge onion, stripped and finely diced
- ◆ 2 carrots, stripped and diced
- ◆ 3 tablespoons extra-virgin olive oil
- ◆ 1 teaspoon caraway seeds, daintily crushed (discretionary)
- ◆ ½ cup whole wheat baked pastry flour
- ◆ 5 cups of water or vegetable stock
- ◆ 1 teaspoon fine grain sea salt, or to taste
- ◆ 14-ounce can cannellini beans, strained and washed

Pesto Herb Dumplings

- ➤ 1 cup almond milk (or whatever milk you like)
- ➤ 1 egg
- ➤ 2 tablespoons pesto
- ➤ 1 cup cleaved herbs (dill, scallions, basil, lemongrass, and so on), plus extra for garnish
- ➤ ½ cup whole wheat baked good flour
- ➤ 2 teaspoons baking powder
- ➤ ½ teaspoon fine grain sea salt

Directions

- In a large, wide soup pot, sauté the onions and carrots in the olive oil over medium-high heat. Cook until the vegetables are delicate, 5-7 minutes. Mix in the caraway seeds, if using, and afterwards sprinkle with the flour, mix, and allow to cook for another 2-3 minutes to enable the flour to toast a tad. Mix in the water and salt, and bring to a delicate boil. Cook until the soup thickens, 5 minutes or thereabouts. Mix in the beans. Permit to stew delicately while you make the dumplings.

- In a blending bowl, consolidate the almond milk, egg, and pesto; whisk well, until uniform, at which point include the herbs. In another mixing bowl, whisk the flour, baking powder, and salt. Empty the fluid ingredients into the dry; mix with a huge fork until combined. Drop liberal tablespoons of this dumpling blend into the delicately stewing soup. Fight the temptation to make the dumplings bigger than this, as they will bloom in size. It's fine if the dumplings are touching. Spread and cook for 7 minutes or thereabouts. Use a large spoon to flip each dumpling, and cook for an additional 7 minutes, or until cooked through. Serve hot, and garnish with chopped herbs and scallions.

Instant Pot Chickpea Cauliflower Korma

Ingredients

- 2 cups Indian-spiced simmer sauce, preferably korma curry sauce
- 2 lb. head of cauliflower, cut into florets
- 1 14-ounce can chickpeas, drained and washed
- 1 14-ounce jar of diced, fire-broiled tomatoes (discretionary)
- 1 small onion, diced
- 4 cloves of garlic, minced
- 1-inch piece of ginger, stripped and ground
- 1 cup cilantro, cleaved

For serving: Lemon olive oil, a squeeze of lemon juice, salted-crushed garlic yoghurt, lemon zest, fresh herbs (cilantro, dill, and so on.)

Directions

> ➢ Empty the sauce into the base of the Instant Pot in an even layer. Include the cauliflower, chickpeas, tomatoes, onion, garlic, and ginger. Give every one of them a tad of a mix, and close the pot. Secure the cover, set the weight discharge valve to sealing. Press manual for 4 minutes at high pressure.

> ➢ When cooking is finished, cautiously quick release. Delicately shake or tap the pressure cooker, and afterwards, cautiously open away from you. Mix in half of the cilantro, and save the rest for serving. Scoop the korma into dishes and include garnishes as you like.

NOTES

To make on an ordinary stovetop, bring the sauce to a boil, mix in the various fixings (aside from cilantro), spread, and cook until the cauliflower is delicate, 5-7 minutes or thereabouts. Continue with the recipe as written.

WINTER GREEN MISO PASTE

The one thing to remember here is that some miso is a lot saltier than others. You can generally add salt to taste, yet it's somewhat harder to go about removing the salt. I'll frequently add a liberal touch to a pot of heated water, include more paste until the flavour is sufficient, and afterwards finish with salt to taste. If the flavours aren't popping, or things are tasting flat, include progressive pinches salt, one at a time. This recipe makes a large amount; store as much as you may use in seven days in the fridge, and put the rest in little baggies, or ice 3D square plate, for the freezer. If you are staying away from soy, search out chickpea or other non-soy miso.

Ingredients

- ½ cup natural miso
- ⅔ cup extra virgin olive oil
- 4 medium cloves of garlic, stripped
- 2 tablespoons crisp rosemary
- 2 bunches of cilantro, leaves and stems
- 16 scallions, cut
- 2-inch fragment of ginger, stripped

Directions

- ➤ Use a food processor or blender to puree all fixings into a paste. Taste, alter flavorings accordingly, and use.

NOTES

Makes around 2 cups.

To make the pictured noodle bowl, make a simple pot of wintergreen miso soup. Cook noodles, and include some broccoli last. Strain. Broil miso-slathered tofu (as well as veggies) in a 375°F stove until well done. Arrange noodles, broccoli, and tofu in bowls, pour miso soup over it all, and finish with hemp seeds and bunches of chives. Enjoy!

Instant Pot Minestrone Soup

Ingredients

- 2 tablespoons extra virgin olive oil
- 1 medium onion, diced
- 3 carrots, cut into ¼-inch coins
- 3 celery stalks, diced
- 2 medium cloves garlic, minced
- 1 teaspoon crushed red chili pepper
- ½ cups dried cannellini beans
- 5 medium waxy potatoes, the size of an egg, divided
- 3-inch lump of Parmesan skin (discretionary)
- 8 cups water
- 1 medium bundle of kale or chard, de-stemmed and cleaved

- ¼ cup crushed tomatoes, from can
- 1 teaspoon fine grain sea salt

Discretionary garnish suggestions: Chopped dark olives, a touch of pesto, a shower of lemon olive oil, or a large squeeze of lemon juice

Directions

> Press the saute on the Instant Pot, and press it again to knock it to saute more. Warm the olive oil in the Instant Pot, then sauté the onion, carrots, celery, and garlic until mollified, 5-7 minutes. Mix in the chili chips, beans, potatoes, Parmesan skin (if using), and 8 cups of water. Press cancel.

> Close and seal the pot, and weight cook on manual for 40 minutes* (high). Cautiously press quick release when finished. Delicately shake or tap the pressure cooker, and afterwards, cautiously open it away from you. Remove the Parmesan skin, and tenderly mix in the salt. Taste and alter with more if necessary. Mix in the kale, and once it has integrated, mix in the tomatoes. Serve as-is, or with sliced olives and a dusting of cheddar.

NOTES

*If after 40 minutes your beans aren't cooked through and you have the opportunity, simply adequately cook them, covered, exactly as you would prefer. They ought to be close with this advice, yet you never know! The age and nature of dried beans shifts drastically. Then again, you can reseal the IP and go for another 5 or 10 minutes.

Vegetable Noodle Soup

Use whatever short pasta you like here. Then again, you can use angel hair pasta broken into short sections, or long, plump udon noodles. It is difficult to make this dish turn out badly. If you don't have dietary yeast available (and wouldn't fret about a touch of cheese), you can grind some Parmesan over each bowl.

Ingredients

- 12 ounces extra-firm tofu, patted dry with paper towels and cut into ¼-inch cubes
- ½ tablespoons extra virgin olive oil
- 4 cloves garlic, cleaved
- 1 medium onion, finely cleaved

- 1 cup carrots, finely cleaved
- 2 cups celery, finely cleaved
- ¼ teaspoon dried turmeric
- 1 tablespoon thyme leaves (new or dried)
- 1 teaspoon oregano (new or dried)
- 1 bay leaf
- Salt and pepper to taste
- ½ tablespoons healthful yeast (or see headnotes)
- 8 cups water
- 12 ounces dried pasta, cooked per bundle directions
- **To serve:** fresh cilantro, cleaved kale, slashed chives

Directions

➢ Heat the stove to 375°F, toss the tofu with ½ tablespoon of the olive oil, place on a lined baking sheet, and cook 15 minutes, or until somewhat brilliant in shading. Move the tofu to a bowl, and put in a safe spot.

➢ Warm the remaining 1 tablespoon of olive oil in a large soup pot over medium-high heat. Include the garlic, onion, carrots, and celery, and sauté for 10 minutes, just until the onions begin to take on a touch of shading. Include the turmeric, thyme, oregano, bay leaf, 1 teaspoon of salt, dietary yeast, and some freshly ground pepper. Add the water and bring to a boil. Taste the juices and include more salt and pepper if needed. Don't under salt, or the soup will taste dismal and bland.

> I like to cook the pasta independently, as it just keeps the juices cleaner and more brilliant, but you can surely cook it in the broth*. In any case, add the pasta in now. If you haven't pre-cooked the noodles, boil until cooked through, mix in the tofu, and serve the noodle soup extra hot, in singular dishes, topped with heaps of fresh cilantro or chives, or cleaved kale for added greens.

NOTES

*If you cook the pasta with the remainder of the soup, you may need to include additional water and re-season.

Caramelised Tofu

Any extra-firm tofu will work here, but attempt to buy organic, non-GMO tofu. Additionally, if you don't relish cilantro, don't hesitate to swap in pea shoots, or even thinly sliced kale.

Ingredients

- 7-8 ounces extra-firm tofu, cut into slight 1-inch sections
- Several pinches of fine-grain sea salt
- Several sprinkles of olive oil
- 2 medium cloves garlic, minced
- ⅓ cup walnuts, toasted and cleaved

- 3 tablespoons fine-grain regular pure sweetener or brown sugar
- ¼ cup cilantro, cleaved
- ½ lb. Brussels sprouts, washed and cut into 1/8-inch wide strips

Directions

➤ Cook the tofu strips in the hot skillet or pot with a touch of salt and a sprinkle of oil. Sauté until somewhat brown, around 4 minutes. Include the garlic and walnuts, and cook for one more moment. Mix in sugar. Cook for another couple of minutes. Remove from heat and mix in the cilantro. Scratch the tofu out onto a plate and put in a safe spot while you cook the Brussels sprouts.

➤ In the same container (no compelling reason to wash), include a touch more oil, another spot of salt, and dial the heat up to medium-high. When the dish is pleasant and hot, mix in the shredded Brussels sprouts. Cook for 2-3 minutes, blending a handful of times until you get some golden bits, and the remainders of the sprouts are splendid and scrumptious.

GOTH HUMMUS

Poke around on the Internet and at specialty food stores for black garbanzos (look in bulk, and with other dried beans). If you find them, stock up — this hummus turns out well outside of Halloween!

Ingredients

- ◆ 4 cups cooked dark garbanzos, plus additional for serving
- ◆ 4-6 tablespoons lemon juice
- ◆ 4 medium garlic cloves (black, discretionary)
- ◆ 1½ teaspoon fine grain sea salt
- ◆ 1 cup dark tahini, plus 1 tablespoon
- ◆ 1 cup super-cold water

- 2 tablespoons extra virgin olive oil
- **To serve**: edible flowers (sage, chive, thyme, and so forth), and sesame seeds

Directions

In a blender or food processor, puree the chickpeas into a thick paste. Include the lemon juice, garlic, and salt. With the processor running, include the tahini. Gradually rinse in the super cold water. Continue handling for about 4-5 minutes. Taste and modify.

California Tom Yum Soup

This comes together rapidly once you have everything cleaved, so make certain to have everything slashed and prepared before you start cooking.

Ingredients

- ♦ 8 cups of water
- ♦ 2 large Roma tomatoes (cut in 1/6ths), or 20 cherry tomatoes (divided)
- ♦ 2 dried guajillo chili peppers, coarsely chopped
- ♦ ½ tablespoons palm, muscovado, or brown sugar
- ♦ 1 serving of Tom Yum Paste*
- ♦ 8-12 ounces blended mushrooms (nameko, shellfish, and so forth)

- A sprinkle of shoyu or soy sauce, to taste
- ⅓ cup fresh lime juice, or to taste
- ¼ cup chopped cilantro in each bowl, for serving

To serve: Serve with lime wedges, steamed rice, and warm tofu. Extra points for a shower of lemon olive oil, lime oil, and/or broiled cherry tomatoes.

Instructions

- ➢ Heat the water to the point of boiling in a medium pan. Add the tomatoes, Guajillo chili, and sugar. Stew for a couple of moments, until the tomato relaxes, and then add the Tom Yum Paste*.
- ➢ Permit to stew for a moment or two, before adding the mushrooms. Stew until delicate. Include a little sprinkle of shoyu or soy sauce, and a bit of the lime juice. Taste, and change with a greater amount of either, if necessary. Spot ¼ cup of slashed cilantro in the base of each bowl, and top with the soup.

Five-Minute Avocado Dressing with Herbs and Spinach

I know a great deal of you keep spinach in the freezer for smoothies — use that! On the off chance that you don't have miso, just salt to taste.

Ingredients

- ½ medium ripe avocado, (~½ cup)
- 1 cup nut milk (almond, cashew, and so on), plus extra to thin if necessary
- 1 cup spinach (frozen is alright)
- ½ tablespoon fresh herbs (thyme, oregano)
- 3 cloves garlic, stripped
- 1 teaspoon miso, to taste

- 1-2 tablespoons fresh lemon juice

Directions

> Consolidate the avocado, nut milk, spinach, herbs, garlic, miso, and 1 tablespoon of the lemon juice. Thin with more milk to make the dressing pourable. Taste, and add more lemon juice as well as a touch of salt to season to taste.

Coconut Red Lentil Soup

The primary recipe if you aren't sure what sort of lentils and split peas to purchase. For those of you who are interested, I used the Terre Exotique Madras Curry Powder. I got it in Paris. But it would appear that it is accessible here now as well (I suspect I've gone over it on Amazon's basic food item area). Veggie lovers — you can without much of a stretch make this vegan by using coconut or olive oil instead of the margarine called for.

Instructions

- ◆ 1 cup (7 oz) yellow split peas
- ◆ 1 cup (7 oz) red split lentils (masoor dal)
- ◆ 7 cups water

- 1 medium carrot, diced into ½-inch cubes
- 2 tablespoons fresh stripped and minced ginger
- 2 tablespoons curry powder
- 2 tablespoons margarine spread, ghee, or coconut oil
- 8 green onions or scallions, daintily cut
- 3 tablespoons golden raisins
- ⅓ cup tomato paste
- 1 14-ounce can coconut milk
- 2 teaspoons fine-grain sea salt
- 1 small bunch cilantro, cleaved

Directions

- Give the split peas and lentils a good flush until they never again put off colored water. Put them in an extra-large soup pot, fill with the water, and heat to the point of boiling. Diminish heat to a stew and add the carrot and a quarter of the ginger. Mix and stew for around 30 minutes, or until the split peas are delicate.
- Meanwhile, in a small dry skillet or pot over low warmth, toast the curry powder until it is very fragrant. Be cautious, however; if you would prefer not to inhale the curry powder, toast it. Put in a safe spot.
- Spot the spread in a dish over medium heat, include half of the green onions, the remaining ginger, and raisins. Sauté for 2 minutes blending continually, then at that point include the tomato paste and sauté for 1-2 moments.

➤ Add the toasted curry powder to the tomato paste blend, blend well, and afterwards add this to the stewing soup alongside the coconut milk and salt. Stew uncovered for 20 minutes or so. The surface ought to thicken up, but you can mess with the consistency if you like by including more water, or on the other hand stew it longer for a thicker consistency. Personally, the thicker this soup got, the more I preferred it.

➤ I've been getting a kick out of serving scoops of this soup over ~½ cup of warm farro (extra from my Farro and Bean Stew). Dark colored rice was great also. Sprinkle each bowl liberally with cilantro and the remaining green onions.

NOTES

Instant Pot variety: For Instant Pot clients, one of you (thanks Andrea!) kept in touch with me and said this soup works incredibly in the IP: sauté the zest, onions, tomato paste, ginger, and raisins. Include the lentils, split, peas, ginger, carrot, and water and cook on high weight for 15 minutes with a characteristic discharge. At that point, I include coconut milk.

Printed in Great Britain
by Amazon